How to Create an Unlimited Income
Sitting at Home in Your Pajamas

By Michael Klisouris

PublishAmerica
Baltimore

© 2005 by Michael Klisouris.

All rights reserved. No part of this book may be reproduced, stored in a retrieval system, or transmitted in any form or by any means without the prior written permission of the publishers, except by a reviewer who may quote brief passages in a review to be printed in a newspaper, magazine, or journal.

First printing

ISBN: 1-4137-9026-7
PUBLISHED BY PUBLISHAMERICA, LLLP
www.publishamerica.com
Baltimore

Printed in the United States of America

I wish to dedicate this book to two people who have touched my heart and soul in so many ways. The first person being my beloved mother, Voula Klisouris, who passed away a number of years back. One of the things she taught me was to always follow my passions, and this book is proof thereof.
The second person worthy of dedication is my girlfriend, Annette Shand. Her loving personality and unlimited support will never be duplicated.
You are my true wealth...I love you both.

Introduction

As you embrace this open book, opportunity is beckoning you to take her by the hand so she can lead you to prosperity.

There are countless reasons why you are seeking her guidance. The world and our economy are constantly changing. Corporate downsizing abounds, job security is definitely a thing of the past. Your employer does not provide you with the creative work environment you so long for, the daily two-hour commute eats away at your valuable family time, and your dwindling raises and fixed income are losing pace against yearly inflation. You are tired of the office politics and the water-cooler gossip. Deep down inside you know there is a better way than this rat-race!

Now imagine a different scenario. You have a five-second commute from your bedroom into your home-office. You are not racing against any other rats – **AS YOU ARE NOW THE KING RODENT**. You spend a leisurely day in your pajamas, earning an income which has no ceiling. You choose your hours, you pick your breaks. You work in a field that you are passionate about. Getting fired and losing your one source of income is no longer a worry, as you have hundreds of client–income streams pouring in. Your family is just a stone's throw away, making it easy to balance your work and home life. You are healthier because your refrigerator, full of healthy foods, is 30 paces from your desk and your home gym is down a flight of stairs to the basement. But most importantly, you have freedom. The freedom **TO DO WHAT YOU WANT, WHEN YOU WANT TO.** You are in control of your own destiny. Now this is living!

My ultimate goal in writing this book is to provide you with the ideas, systems, and motivation to create a home-entrepreneur lifestyle as depicted above. The information presented is a cumulative effort of my own 17 years of business experiences (both failures and successes revealed), wealthy mentor contacts, as well as an exhaustive research of the most financially successful individuals throughout history. My studies and business background have allowed me to discover a set of common methods, characteristics and strategies, which I hope you will use to create your own personal success. It's important to know that these strategies have been implemented by many of my corporate clients over and over again, to the tune of selling millions of dollars worth of products and services. If followed sensibly and consistently, many of these systems and tips should work for you as well!

Through the pages of this book, you will encounter the most eye-opening and sometimes unorthodox ideas to stimulate your mind and take you to levels of finance you never dreamed of before. Make no mistake, there are no get-rich-quick schemes presented in these pages, only time-tested and proven systems guaranteed to help you build a thriving home-based direct marketing business. The ideas can be implemented on a part-time basis while you are still employed at your full-time job. Once a sustainable level of success is reached, you can quit your dreary job and run your exciting new business from the comfort of your home. All the ideas take into account that most readers do not have thousands to invest up-front in a business opportunity. Hence, all the presented systems can be implemented on a shoestring budget. No immense product inventories, or employee labor is required. Most of the ideas can be turned into thriving money trees, capable of flowering income without the owner being present to oversee the day-to-day operations.

It is my intent to create a writing format of small, detailed paragraphs packed with easy-to-understand language. Step-by-step instructions have been written where possible to keep everything short, simple and with laser focus. Lengthy explanations are used only at times of utmost importance, and when messages have to be backed up with real life examples.

In Part 1, you will discover the advice and tips required in building a solid foundation prior to reading my remaining information. Part 2 will take you into the meat-and-potatoes activities of creating and running a profitable direct marking business from home. In this section you will learn what works, what doesn't, and why. I added Part 3 for those individuals interested in taking their home business to higher levels of income, responsibility, and growing it into a larger and more complex organization. Purposely, I cover a wide topic of interests, including business, finances, relationships, management, investments, marketing, expansion, and others. My reasoning for this was that I wanted to create an all-around **SUCCESS MANUAL** appealing to a general audience.

*HOW TO CREATE AN UNLIMITED INCOME
SITTING AT HOME IN YOUR PAJAMAS*

Readers absorbing my information will be able to bend it, mold it, and tailor it to fit into many varied situations, businesses and life circumstances.

So grasp opportunity by the arm as she leads you into the unknown. She will guide you to financial freedom and unlimited income, sitting at home in your pajamas!

Part 1

Chapter 1
Success Tips

SUCCESS TIP #1 – CREATE A MASTER PLAN

It is a well-known fact that the people who have taken the time to create written goals achieve more in life. Now don't get me wrong here, I'm not saying that if you write down your goals you will immediately achieve sudden success. But it sure does help. Surveys have been performed, and findings indicate that the 3% of candidates who did create a "master plan" went on to surpass the remaining 97% who did not have any written goals! Look at it this way: you will be taking a journey into uncharted territory as you extend your mind and actions to create something new for yourself. How will you know if you are on track or if you are off course from reaching your desired goals, if nothing is written down on paper?

Following is a step-by-step format for creating your "master plan." After reading my book, you will have a mind full of practical ideas you can begin to implement. It is at this point that you should immediately begin to follow these steps.

Record your goals/dreams down on paper. Purchase a notebook you will be comfortable using, and take one hour to think carefully of what you want in life. Let your imagination run wild and begin writing down everything. Goals should extend into all areas of your life, creating a well-balanced structure: financial, spiritual, leisure, friends, family, social, mental, physical, etc. Keep writing until you have at least five goals for each category.

Your goals must coincide with your values. Values are feelings, things, or people of utmost importance to you. Have you ever noticed celebrities who have reached immense financial success, only to have it all crumble beneath them due to a suicide, arrest, or addiction of some kind? This is a perfect example of someone reaching out, due to an emptiness of values not being on the same line as their goals.

Establish a firm date when you will accomplish your goals. Make sure your goals are believable, attainable, and can be reached within a concise and measurable time frame. It is ludicrous to believe you can earn $100,000 in January, when you only earned $5,000 in December.

Create a daily plan immediately to reach your goals and dreams. As noted above, after you have read my book, you will have hundreds of incredible ideas you can use to match up your values. Write your daily plan down right away!

Take action instantly to put your plan into practice. Do not lose any time hesitating. You must move forward enthusiastically while your plans are fresh and exciting.

Study your goals on a daily basis. I would suggest going over your dreams/goals at least twice a day. Once in the morning, and then again before retiring to bed in the evening. Imagine yourself already having achieved your goals. At the end of the day, re-cap your daily activities to see if they have assisted you in moving closer to your goals.

Have the flexibility to modify your plans. If you feel that you are banging your head against the wall, and not moving forward, then this is an indication that your plans are not solid. Replace these plans with new ones. Your goal (destination) will remain the same, only your direction will change. This is where most people procrastinate and give up at the first sign of an obstacle. Get past this sticking point by having alternate plans ready in the back of your mind at all times.

Pit-bull persistence never fails. Have you ever seen a pit-bull bite down and lock his jaws? You can beat him with baseball bat and he won't let go! This is exactly how you should be. Just don't quit…ever. Keep making new plans and putting them into action, until you find one that works. Edison failed over 10,000 times before he created the light bulb. If Edison had been a quitter, you'd be reading this book beside a burning fire as your source of light! So powerful is this character trait of "persistence" that I have allocated it a section later in my book.

One more word of advice—as you achieve your goals and dreams, always have a few new ones written down to take the place of the ones you cross off your list, this way you will be in a constant state of improvement!

SUCCESS TIP #2 – TAKE THE ROAD LESS TRAVELED

I'm sure you have heard of the poem by Robert Frost where this title comes from. Mr. Frost ends his poem by saying "I took the one less traveled by, and that has made all the difference." His writing perfectly describes the bucking of the norm, the breaking of the mold and the moving forward into new and uncharted directions. Look around you at the masses with a critical eye and examine carefully their habits and their actions. Entrepreneurs are by nature hands-on risk-takers. You, in turn, must be willing to look at the crowd and move in the opposite direction. If friends and acquaintances are working at 9 to 5 dead-end jobs, you start your own business. If others are buying consumer items on credit and going into debt, you save and pay with cash. If the masses are buying one home and taking 25 years to pay it off, you buy five houses and have them all mortgage free in 15 years!

Question the use of savings accounts, RRSP's, mortgages, investing, time management, thoughts and beliefs, as thinking differently on these and other matters will greatly affect the outcome of your future. We will delve deeper on these issues as you read along. For now, try to adapt this new way of thinking. Do something opposite from the norm. Tomorrow, get dressed and go out without any underwear underneath! Break your habits! I often wake up at 4 a.m. and find the solitude of the morning to be very inspiring, and this helps me to be incredibly productive. Are you willing to do the same?

So keep an open mind to change and stay focused on that "road less traveled." Always remember: in order to achieve a level of financial greatness, you have to be willing to do what most people are not willing to do…and this many times means being a contrarian.

SUCCESS TIP #3 – CHANGE YOUR THOUGHTS AND YOUR LIFE

Think about this for a moment: Your thoughts, decisions, and actions have brought you to where you are today. Do you know that the combined decisions you made in the past have affected the lifestyle you are presently living? In other words, adding up all your life's decisions will equal the life you now enjoy.

The funny thing is you have complete control over your thoughts, and the full freedom to think as you choose. Does it not make sense then that if we can control our thoughts and eventually our actions, then why not be optimistic and hold a positive mental attitude at all times? The mind is a powerful entity, and we use about 10% of its full potential. No man-made computer can even come close to matching the complexity of the human brain.

Get into the habit of holding only positive thoughts in your mind at all times. You will find this hard to do, as our default subconscious always "sneaks" in a few negatives here and there. Don't question nagging doubts or self-limiting beliefs. Don't dwell more than 10% on a problem, but right away spend 90% thinking of a solution. Whatever you believe in with full emotion, will eventually become your reality in the future.

Above all, don't blame others for where you are today. Don't blame your government, your boss, your parents, luck, your educational background, your intelligence, the right contacts or your health for the way your life has materialized. Blame only your thoughts, and take an active approach in changing them.

SUCCESS TIP #4 – LONG HOURS ARE A GIVEN

History books are littered with hundreds of titans of wealth who displayed immense drive, energy, determination, and long work hours. J. Paul Getty went days without sleeping as he worked around the clock. Bill Gates held contests with his college buddies to see how long they could work nonstop—sometimes without showering for days! Sixteen–, eighteen– and twenty–hour work days were the norm for these and many other billionaires.

I hope I'm not scaring you here. To build a successful enterprise of any kind will definitely require you to put in longer than the usual 40-hour work week. There is just no getting around this. If you work regular hours, you will receive a regular employee pay-check. If you increase the quality and quantity of the service/product you provide, a higher level of financial success will ultimately be yours.

In the beginning stages of a business, where you are researching or creating your product and/or service, you will have to put in above average work hours. Later, with the business in place and showing a nice profit, you can cut your work hours down to a comfortable level. It's interesting to note that entrepreneurs are willing to work 70 hours a week for themselves so they don't have to work 35 hours for somebody else!

SUCCESS TIP# 5 – GET IN SHAPE

It consistently blows my mind when I think about it. We have only one body in this lifetime, and we do so much to abuse it. A small investment on a daily basis will help you reap many benefits now and in the future. One of these small investments is exercising on a consistent basis. The benefits are too long to mention here, some of which are: increased energy, a longer life and fewer medical bills. It is pointless to create all this financial abundance so that you can become the richest person in the hospital!

I don't care who you are and how many responsibilities you have, everyone can find a half–hour on a daily basis to do some form of exercise. Make it part of your life and write it in your daily calendar (buy one if you don't have one already). You eat, you go to the bathroom, you sleep, and so you must exercise. Make it a habit. Psychologists agree that rats can acquire a new behavior in about 30 repetitions. So in 30 days you should have the habit of exercise embedded in your brain!

I personally have been exercising consistently for 20 years now, and I very rarely miss my workouts, as they are embedded in my brain as part of my daily activities. I train for 1 to 1.5 hours five or six days per week. For those of you groaning right now, I offer these small words of advice:

- **Create a gym in your home.** Furnish it with equipment that can be bought for pennies on the dollar at garage sales. Having a gym at home makes it extremely convenient to exercise at odd hours, and hours which better suit your schedule. It also saves plenty of time—which you can use to market your new business!
- **Start off with a half–hour a day.** If you are a beginner, start off with half an hour, three times a week and work up from there. Increase your workout

times and days until you find a comfortable level. Every person is different, so find what works best for you in sustaining a healthier lifestyle. An advanced fitness buff can do one-hour workouts, six days a week. Make sure that you are sweating and your heart is pumping when you are working out. This will indicate that you are exercising at an effective intensity.

- **Vary your workouts.** Add stretching, aerobic and weight training into your workouts to combine and alternate and keep your training interesting and fresh. You might even want to try kick-boxing, yoga, or jogging. Lift heavy weights one day and light weights the next. Add explosive, quick bursts of energy (about 1 or 2 minutes long) into your aerobic workouts. Alternate the order of your exercises as well. When muscles get used to the same routine, you will begin to see minimum results, so change up your routine for constant improvements.
- **Break up your workouts.** Try this trick used by professional bodybuilders: Do two workouts, one in the morning and one in the late afternoon or early evening. Aerobics are best done on an empty stomach in the morning, and this is when you will get the best results. Do your weights and/or stretching as your second workout. Research indicates that breaking up your workouts produces the same results as doing one complete long workout.
- **Streamline your workouts.** When doing weight training, after you finish one set of an exercise, immediately begin a set of an opposing muscle group exercise. For example: finish a set of bench presses (for the chest) and immediately move to a leg press exercise. In this fashion, when you are resting your one muscle group, you are working another. This tip can cut your workouts to half the time. It also makes your workouts more aerobic in nature, therefore causing you to burn more calories.
- **Slow, controlled movements.** When weight training, move in a slow and controlled movement, do not swing the weights. Pause for two seconds at the top of the movement. Pay close attention to the lowering part of the exercise, as research indicates that the declining phase of an exercise is just as important as the raising phase in building muscle.
- **Other health tips:** Drink eight glasses of water on a daily basis. Eat five or six small meals a day, as this helps the body in breaking down the nutrients in your food better and also increases metabolism. Take daily vitamins and supplements. Get plenty of rest – at least seven hours of sleep each night (as the body changes when you rest, not when you workout). Eat chicken, tuna, turkey and fish as your main protein sources. Eat more fruits and vegetables.

Eliminate all fast foods, fried or baked goods, chocolates, candies and chips. Throw in one cheat day (come on, no one is perfect!) where you can eat your favorite junk foods.

Furthermore, on the subject of weight loss…try this two-fold tip: #1. Put fewer calories into your mouth, and #2. Get off the couch and exercise more! Trust me, you will lose weight!

SUCCESS TIP #6 – KILL THE DUMB BOX

Did you figure out what the dumb box is? It is the television. It boggles my mind knowing that the average American watches over 30 hours of television every week. With the destruction on September 11, many people are spending more time at home with their families. Trends are moving towards and centering around the home. Home entertainment, home theatre systems, wide-screens, HDTV, plasma TV's—these are all huge at the time of this writing.

All I have to say is this: knowing that money represents service, the more service you can give, the more money you will learn. Sitting in a trance, watching sitcoms on TV does not in any way **MOVE YOU ANY CLOSER TO YOUR GOALS AND DREAMS.** About the only thing it does is it helps the television networks and actors become rich!

Find valuable time by eliminating television watching nearly completely from your daily life. I say "NEARLY" completely because there are a few shows and educational programs which you may still want to watch, as they will benefit you indirectly. Things like biographies of successful individuals, infomercials (to pick up on how products are marketed), the weather and the daily news, these are all excellent programs to watch. I would say half to one hour a day of television is more than enough to relax and wind down after a hard day at your home office!

SUCCESS TIP #7 – ELIMINATE DAILY CHORES

There are many activities which we perform on a daily basis which do not contribute in any way whatsoever to our daily goals. A few of these are cooking, doing dishes, vacuuming, washing the car, paying the bills, doing laundry, cutting the grass, home maintenance and repairs, maintaining your vehicle, grocery shopping, etc. etc. The list can go on almost unending. Do you get the drift?

These items have to get done, it is a matter of existing that we have to perform these boring duties...but we don't have to necessarily do them ourselves!

Think of it this way. If you develop a business that earns you an hourly pay of $100 an hour (not uncommon with the ideas I will be teaching you), and you perform 10 hours a week of daily chores, then you are actually spending $1,000 of **YOUR VALUE** each week. Does it not make sense to hire an assistant, cleaning lady or kid from the neighbourhood, for $10/hour ($100 each week) to do all these extra chores for you? Imagine the time you will save, which you can in turn use to build your businesses, spend with your friends/family, and improve the overall quality of your life!

I have a personal assistant who comes over every weekend and does my shopping, cleaning, and even cooks all my weekly meals and freezes them in plastic containers for me! During the week, when I am working hard, I pop a container in the microwave and have a healthy and quick meal within minutes. Internet grocery delivery services are an excellent idea to save time on shopping.

Simple chores like washing the car, gardening, cutting the grass, and snow shoveling can be given to your children or relatives' children as a method of demonstrating the value of "earning their own way."

Take this excellent bit of advice and hire out as much as you can. The small investment you will pay will truly enrich your life by providing you with many hours of new found time.

SUCCESS TIP #8 – MAINTAINING CONTROL

In every aspect of your life, do your best to maintain control and ownership and you will create ultimate freedom. Own your home—don't rent; create your own business and sign the paycheck you desire, buy your car cash—don't lease or finance. Manage your own investments and reap a mountain of profits. It makes no sense to play by someone else's rules, as you will become frustrated and unable to make the changes necessary to improve your life. Why fight and claw your way up the corporate ladder, when you can start your own business and buy your own ladder!

Nobody will care for your money as much as you will. Think carefully about letting others manage or control your finances. The outcome can sometimes be disastrous.

*HOW TO CREATE AN UNLIMITED INCOME
SITTING AT HOME IN YOUR PAJAMAS*

In fact, I would not let anyone guide me financially, unless they personally have achieved the success or results which I am searching for. If you wish to become a millionaire, then don't ask your friends, family, or a bum on the street for financial advice—ask a millionaire. With investments like stocks, commodities, and mutual funds, it feels almost like playing Russian Roulette...you never know when you will have to bite the bullet!

Ownership of one's own business offers the most flexibility and control than any other investment vehicle. You own the service or product you have created, you decide how to market it, how to manage it, how to expand on it, when to hire and fire employees, and so on. There is no greater feeling on earth than being in control of your own destiny, and this should be at the top of your goals list!

SUCCESS TIP #9 – WEALTH BUILDING RATES OF RETURN

Here is a secret all millionaires know, but neglect to spread the word to the rest of the population. **Do not finance any investment which does not give you a rate of return of 100% or more.** Have you ever read in *Forbes* magazine the way the richest people in America made their money? Did you ever notice savings accounts, GIC's, RRSP's or employee salary as their prime wealth vehicle? I rest my case.

Following is a small example to teach you about compounding at wealth–building rates of return. If I was to offer you a freelance job lasting 30 days, and I gave the choice of receiving a pay of $1,000 a day or a penny a day compounded daily at a rate of return of 100%...which would you choose? Would you select the penny a day because you feel like I'm trying to pull a fast one on you? Do you know why the penny a day is the wise choice? Because if you took the $1,000/day pay, after 30 days you would end up with $30,000 (which is not a bad monthly pay). If you would have taken the penny-a-day compounded at 100%, after 30 days you would have $5,368,709.12—over 5 million dollars! The benefits of compounding can be truly mind-boggling, but don't forget one extremely important fact: **YOU MUST GIVE IT TIME TO WORK.** You should always be looking at investments as long-term, never speculating, or jumping in and out of markets. Imitate our friend Warren Buffett and be a wise buy-and-hold investor.

Many of America's most successful individuals earn 100%, 200%, 1,000%, 2,000%, and even more on a continuous and yearly basis. As you read on, we will cover the methods and systems which will allow you to do the same thing. For now just make a mental note not to conform to the masses in their investment choices, and to have the mind-set in place to create your own wealth–building rates of return.

SUCCESS TIP #10 – YOU CAN'T TAKE IT WITH YOU

Money, money, money, it's all we seem to be talking about. Don't worry, there are many other important subjects in life, and we will be covering those subjects as well. But for now, think this interesting thought over: We come into the world broke, and we will die broke. Money only flows to us temporary while we are here on earth. So make sure to enjoy some of it while you are alive and healthy! And also remember, that when it comes to money you can do only four things with it:

Save It
Invest It
Lend It
Spend It

Don't make money a means to an end. It is not everything in life, and I can prove it to you. I will give you a million dollars right now! How does that feel…are you happy? Oh, I forgot to mention one little catch though—you can have the million dollars in a huge crate in $100 bills, but I will drop this crate off on an uncharted remote tropical island where you have to spend the rest of your life there with your money. You cannot have your girlfriend, your wife, your children, your brothers, your sisters, your favorite pet…NONE OF THEM…you have to leave everyone behind. How do you feel now? Can you go through with it? Take some silent time and think about money, how you enjoy it and what it means to you.

SUCCESS TIP #11 – FAMILY STRESS

On the road to financial self-reliance you will become aware that the dogged determination, long hours, financial risks, tremendous energy and focus requirements will take a huge toll on your family life. Be prepared for this and know that certain conflicts will arise. A happy marriage is one of the things which money can't buy. There are countless millionaires who have suffered through numerous divorces only to realize the reason for this is that their mates took a backseat to their business endeavors.

One wealthy titan actually worked in the morning and afternoon of his wedding day, so as not to deviate from his work schedule! Make sure to add some family and social time into your daily activities plans and stick to these appointments as you do your business duties.

SUCCESS TIP #12 - HIGH-STATUS MATERIAL POSSESSIONS

Care should be taken to not conform with the Joneses! If you have to purchase the "imitations of wealth"—brand new exotic vehicles, furs, expensive furniture, yachts, televisions, stereos, recreational vehicles—always purchase these items with cash, **NEVER WITH BORROWED FUNDS.** Make it a habit to invest your cash only in assets that appreciate in value. All consumer items go down as soon as you walk out of the store, and with interest charges added on top, you are slowly digging your own consumer debt grave. Forget about instant gratification, and do what your grandparents taught you—**SACRIFICE TO SAVE AND THEN PAY CASH!**

Purchasing of vehicles is a very important arena. Do your best to always pay cash. Try buying an older "classic" (20-30 years old), such as a Mercedes Benz, Porsche, or Jaguar. As a home-entrepreneur you will probably be driving on rare occasions anyway, and you may be putting only 5,000-10,000 kilometers on the vehicle on a yearly basis. You will be pleasantly surprised to find out that the auto may actually appreciate in value during the time that you own it.

SUCCESS TIP #13 – INTELLIGENCE AND EDUCATION

Did you know that a large percentage of the wealthiest people in America are college dropouts? It is an interesting fact that many of them didn't even finish high school. Funny, they don't have "Wealth 101" in the school systems. Nobody in high school, college or university teaches you to become wealthy. In fact, most teachers are crazy about instructing students on "SECURITY" to become specialists in a certain field and land a job as a salaried employee.

The world is filled with educated and intelligent derelicts. Be sure of one fact: a great idea, well-defined goals, a burning desire, sound plans, and lots of hard work is the key to financial success. A high I.Q. is not a prerequisite; it may help, but it is not necessarily required.

In addition, I feel strongly that you should be focusing on your individuality, your imagination, your resourcefulness, your creativity—and not your intelligence or your education level. I hope all the educators (teachers/professors) out there don't come after me with wooden stakes!

On the subject of education, I would also like to conclude with the following: I have always believed that it is easier to place a small employment ad and hire the credentials or the specialized knowledge which my businesses require. Why would I spend countless years myself acquiring a diploma or certificate? It's actually quite simple. If you would like to start a plumbing service, for example, place an ad and hire a licensed plumber. Thinking of an electrical contracting company? Hire a licensed electrician. As long as you have a passion and a basic understanding of a business you wish to start, hiring the talent is extremely easy. You can be sure that there is never a lack of eager, educated candidates searching for a salary.

SUCCESS TIP #14 – IT'S WHAT YOU KEEP THAT COUNTS

It is interesting to watch the behaviour of most people when I remind them that in their lifetime they will have all earned over a million dollars. Everyone has the earning potential to make a lot of money in their lives, but little resources or knowledge on how to hang on to these funds. Ironically, it is a well-known fact that most of the lucky few who have won lotteries end up after 10 years to be in the same strung-out position as they were prior to their winnings!

A person earning $80,000 a year and spending $75,000 of that is actually not better off than the person earning $40,000 but only living on $20,000, and re-investing the remaining monies in appreciating assets. In the former example, that person earning the high income is playing excellent offence, but poor defense.

The gross earnings of an individual or a company are irrelevant. The bottom dollar (net) amount is the all-important figure. You should know what your fixed monthly expenses are, and you should be able to pull them out of thin air like you can your birth date. Both personal and business expenses must be studied, memorized, and carefully scrutinized for ways to be lowered.

I have personally witnessed large businesses with many employees grossing millions of dollars a year—and the owners being lucky to walk away with $70,000 of remaining dough in their pockets. Many of these owners, finally becoming frustrated by the high overhead, end up downsizing and streamlining their businesses. Many sell their huge office spaces, move the business back to their homes, gross only a fraction of what they used to—but their net profits are incredibly higher. One mentor friend of mine who used to gross 30 million a year and net $70,000, now grosses $600,000 but keeps $400,000 for himself!

Two more destroyers of wealth which bear mentioning here—inflation and taxes. These two are the "silent killers" of your earned and saved funds. You can purchase a GIC earning 14% yearly interest, but inflation is at 11% (most banks will not mention the rate of inflation to you), so when you also factor in your tax bracket, you will actually be in the hole at the end of the tax year. Whether you are investing or building a thriving business, your major goal is always to surpass the rate of taxes and inflation. If you don't heed this advice, you will feel like you are treading water in a pool full of hungry alligators!

SUCCESS TIP #15 – FRUGALITY FACTS

In order to become financially independent one must keep a constant watch over their investments (especially if you've made a bundle and have a lot to lose). Such close and constant scrutiny viewed by onlookers can be mistaken as someone being "stingy," "penny-pincher," or "cheap-skate." I too, have had the liberty of being described in such terms.

After studying successful individuals, I found that a large proportion of them lived in quite modest means. Their homes were not that lavish, they did not drive brand new foreign cars (most drove 10-year-old "junkers" or American pick-up trucks), they walked around in jeans or clothes bought off the rack.

You can't dispute the fact that in order to achieve some noteworthy financial success, you have to be able to save, reinvest and compound your returns. And to be able to save, you have to live below your means! Many success books advertise saving 10% of your earned income and taking it immediately from your paycheque so you don't spend it. I would go as far as say: save as much as you can, probably going as high as 50% of what you earn. This way, you will have a strong dollar base to invest. Aim to be nondescript. Leave the consumption-oriented habits for your neighbours to indulge in.

SUCCESS TIP #16 – THE REALITY OF RRSP'S

Get ready to have your eyes opened wide! Every year (generally between January and February) Canadians are bombarded with advertisements screaming at them to purchase Registered Retirement Savings Plans. The dreams sold here are that enough (tax–free) cash will be saved over the long term, that the investor and his family will live happily ever after in retirement. This is the biggest myth going around in the banking world and here's why:

1. RRSP's are government-regulated, so you have NO SAY where your funds will be invested (I mentioned earlier in my book about having no control—here is a prime example).

2. With RRSP's most of the funds (approximately 75%) will be invested in Canadian-backed investments. This constricts the creative entrepreneur, who is free to seek GLOBAL investments on his own.

3. RRSP's allow you to invest small amounts ($100 to $200 per month) and the maximum contribution limits—this in itself is one of the biggest downfalls, as investors will have a small and very weak principle amount working for him. An entrepreneur is free to invest AS MUCH AS HE WISHES in his investment vehicles. He has the freedom to invest 80 to 90% of his net profits (if he wishes) back into his business—and this will add amazing compounding power to work in his favor.

4. RRSP's take into consideration that the recipient will be at a lower tax bracket when withdrawing the funds later in life and hence his tax payments will be lower. This is really a smoking-mirror, since if one is a wise investor, he/she will probably be in the SAME tax bracket (earning residual income) when he/she retires!

5. RRSP's have no trading worth whatsoever, and you cannot borrow against them. Quite the opposite of an investor's funds, which have "full trading value" allowing for full borrowing power and tax-write-off power.

6. RRSP's will eventually be 100% fully taxable (the tax bite is only temporarily avoided). But if you invest your capital properly and follow other financing methods revealed later in this book, it is possible to pay only 75% of your capital gains in taxes. Furthermore, you will learn that wealthy investors pay only 2-3% of their actual net worth in taxes and how you can do the same.

7. RRSP's generally do not offer the wealth producing rates of return discussed earlier. And this alone will prove insufficient in growing saved RRSP funds into a financially lucrative retirement.

*HOW TO CREATE AN UNLIMITED INCOME
SITTING AT HOME IN YOUR PAJAMAS*

SUCCESS TIP #17 – SAVE A RAINY DAY FUND

Life is full of temporary obstacles, setbacks, pitfalls, problems and frustrations. Get used to it and get over it. Life is not perfect and it never will be. Living from paycheck to paycheck, what would you do if the transmission on your vehicle dies or the furnace on your home quits out on you? Therefore, the savviest of entrepreneurs always has a "rainy day" fund saved for these types of emergencies. You wouldn't want one unforeseen circumstance to wipe you out financially just inches from your big pay-out, would you?

I would recommend saving at least six months of living expenses, prior to heading out on your own entrepreneurial enterprise. This is an extremely healthy and an ideal financial footing to start from. Many members of my audience will not have these funds at the moment, and that is fine. Starting a business on a shoe-string will definitely lower your risks. For a strong and secure financial future, start building your rainy day fund as quickly as feasibly possible.

SUCCESS TIP #18 – THE POWER OF LEVERAGE

Leverage is one of the most powerful forces available for use in creating your own financial empire. Leverage has been used by millionaires and billionaires throughout history and remains a solid principle for wealth accumulation.

What is leverage you ask? Have you ever seen a lever being put to use? A long plank is placed underneath a 2,000 lb. stone, with a base placed very close to the stone, creating a huge handle to force down upon. What ends up happening is you exert a miniscule amount of force, but the results and the outcome are tremendous. A 10-year-old child using this lever can move the 2,000–lb. stone without breaking a sweat!

To further understand the power of leverage, I quote a passage by Archimedes (a great mathematician and scientist): "Give me a lever long enough, and a place to stand, and I can single-handedly move the world."

There are two major leveraging categories which you must master:

MONEY When making investments or building a business, try to borrow as much cash as you can and limit out-laying your own reserves. One example of this is when making real estate investments. If you purchase a $200,000 home and you put $50,000 as a down payment, the home goes up in value to $210,000 after one year – you will have earned an annual rate of return of 20%. But what if you bought this same home with only $10,000 of your own funds? Since you had only 10K of your funds tied up, and the home went up 10K, then you will have realized a 100% return on your invested capital. Now this is leverage at it's best!

PEOPLE Your time is finite, or in other words, a limited resource. Once you run out of hours in a day, it is very difficult to increase your earning potential when you are the sole income-earner! Here is a sample of leveraging people. You create a business placing small classified ads, and find that you require a dispatch center to take the calls. You realize that one dispatch attendant can handle 20 cities and his/her labor can earn you $500/day. Your next goal would be to leverage the dispatchers, and figure out a system to hire and manage as many as you possibly can. If you have four dispatchers taking calls from 80 cities, you will have increased your daily pay up to $2,000!

A word of caution should be emphasized here. Make sure to have a solid system in place first, paying close attention to your base, prior to going insane with your leveraging abilities. Always build on a **SOLID BASE**. This is crucial.

SUCCESS TIP #19 – DAILY BRAIN-FEED

Super-successes make it a habit to constantly improve themselves by reading books, newspapers and magazines on a daily basis. Change is inevitable, it happens on it's own, and in order to keep pace, you have to constantly take an aggressive stance in improving your biggest asset— YOURSELF. This can be accomplished by setting aside at least a half-hour each day for self-improvement. I call this "Brain-Feeding," and this can also include listening to self-improvement tapes, attending seminars, or studying mentors. Any source of material or motivation which adds to your daily advancement is suitable.

Try to improve all areas of your life, not only business. Other areas are: relationships, family, social, spiritual, health/exercise, friendships.

In business, resting on your laurels will cause you to lose your competitive advantage over time. Sooner or later you will find yourself "side-swiped" or having "the rug pulled out from under you" by one of your competitors.

Also try to enhance your creative abilities by engaging in a wide variety of leisure activities such as: listening to different music styles, reading books/magazines containing sectors you are usually not interested in, meeting new contacts, etc, etc.

SUCCESS TIP #20 – YOU CAN'T DO IT ALONE

Entrepreneurs are such a resourceful bunch, that they want to wear all the hats when running a business. They are the service provider, the receptionist, the accountant, the sales and marketing department, the lawyer, the manager, and on and on. I must admit, this is quite feasible at the start-up phase of a new shoe-string business, but due to the inevitable success and growing duties and sales, the business owner will have to inevitably seek assistance.

The point I want to highlight here is to avoid the one-man-show mentality. The main goal of any business is to increase the volume and the quality of a product or service, and always try to do it at a lower production cost. As well, expansion into foreign markets, diversification of product lines, addition of unique services, will all require major help beyond what one person is capable of.

And of course, let's not forget about the customers, since a business cannot and will not exist without them. I'm sure you've heard of the famous saying, "To get what you really want in life, all you have to do is help enough other people get what they want." I strongly believe in this. Being in business also adds the responsibility to society as a whole, stockholders, managers, and principals. As a wealthy individual, you must also feel for an obligation of doing good and giving something back to the public.

So forget about your ideas of a hermit lifestyle, hoarding yourself in your home. If a role model of a home-entrepreneur is what you seek, look no further than Hugh Heffner, the founder of *Playboy*, with his trademark silk pajamas, smoking pipe and gorgeous blonde arm-trophies!

SUCCESS TIP #21 – TIME & LIVING IN THE PRESENT

We all have 24 hours a day for 7 days, or 168 hours of time per week. If you sleep for 8 hours each night, this leaves you with only 16 hours of waking time each day. It is of the utmost importance to realize that you have to make it a goal to be as efficient as you can in this time span. And you should value time. It comes but only once. When we are born, we are actually dying—it's only a matter of time. And it only goes forward, never in reverse. We cannot take a round-trip ticket to the past and change it. So how do you spend your time? How much time do you invest in creating a compelling future?

Don't forget the other activities which will eat away at your precious time. Some of these will be: friends, errands, house chores, hobbies, television, sports/exercise, spouse/mate and your children. Make sure to allocate time in achieving your personal goals and dreams, as well as building the business methods you will be learning from my book.

It is equally important to stay in control of your time and the present moment. Plant a firm footing where you stand, and realize that your present is where you are now and enjoy it to the fullest. Do not allow unforeseen events, fears, health issues, negative emotions, or time-wasting people to rob you of your time.

Spend your working time enjoying what you do for a living—not dreading every passing second. Learn to work effectively, not necessarily harder. A hundred years from now, no one will really care that you worked 18 hours a day. But in the present moment your family cares dearly about the quality and amount of time you have to invest with them.

One important factor about the past is its irrelevance on affecting the future. Because you did not succeed at something in the past, does not mean you cannot become a success in the future. Don't allow the shackles of your past to hold you back from creating a compelling future. When your alarm clock screams at you tomorrow morning, be grateful that you have been given another day of living to enjoy.

Furthermore, don't put off being happy for sometime in the future. Many people have a strange way of thinking I will be happy when: my children turn into teenagers, I pay off the mortgage, I have no car loan, I retire, my children leave the nest, etc. etc. Don't follow this mentality. Instead, choose to be happy in the present moment.

In conclusion, I leave you with this cute little saying: "Yesterday is history…tomorrow is mystery…today is a gift."

SUCCESS TIP #22 – BIRDS OF A FEATHER FLOCK TOGETHER

I'm sure you have heard of this popular line, but it stands true and correct. You are who you associate with. Your close friends and associates' thought patterns and actions will most likely be very similar to yours. Careful examination will probably also reveal similarities in their habits and their hobbies. It is a fact of human nature that we gravitate towards people that have similar likes and attitudes as ourselves. One of the problems of this phenomenon, since humans take the road of least resistance, is to stifle our creative surroundings by associating with people who do not have the same drive and ambitions as successful entrepreneurs do.

It therefore is a good idea to make an effort to **cultivate new contacts and new friendships** as you make your way closer to your goals and dreams. Now I'm not saying to trash all your lifelong friends, just to put an effort into cultivating successful contacts. Identify a mentor who has succeeded in ways you wish to emulate. Take this person out to lunch, and ask him questions in a non-threatening fashion about the steps he took on his journey to success. Ask him for practical advice that you can use. He will most likely help you by offering insights and a point of view that you would have not thought of on your own.

So here's my closing thought on the subject of friends and mentors: **You can't soar high like an eagle…if you surround yourself with turkeys!**

SUCCESS TIP #23 – CONQUERING FEAR

Fear is one of the most debilitating of human emotions. Fear can be extremely unhealthy, and one of the goals should be in eliminating any fears that may be holding back your full potential. There is an endless list of fears, some of which are: death, illness/disease, heights, insects, snakes, being poor, losing loved ones, public speaking, closed spaces, crowded spaces, water, getting old, flying, the dark, etc.

How many of the above fears to you feel on a regular basis? One strange phenomenon about fear is that in many cases it is event-related. What this means is that as a child something happened to you that caused you to have these fears later on in life. For example, perhaps you were bitten by a dog, so later in life you developed a fear of dogs. Or you fell into a pool at a very young age, so later you realized you feared deep water. I know of a simple method for conquering fear:

Attack Your Fear Head On With Gradual, Step-by-step Action!

Here is the procedure to take if you fear spiders. First start staring at them at books for short periods moving up to longer periods. Then purchase a fake rubber spider and learn to play with it and keep it around you at all times. Finally, find a small live spider and place it in your hand and let it run around freely. You want **gradual action** of some kind, **not cold turkey** action, like going out and picking up a live spider immediately (this would be entirely too overpowering).

Certain fears, like the fear of being poor, cannot be felt or picked up, as they are inanimate feelings. These fears have to be controlled by gradual thought and understanding that these have to be accepted as part of life, of living, getting old, losing loved ones, having less wealth, and eventually dying.

SUCCESS TIP #24 – DESTROYING WORRY

Worry is another self-destructive and sometime crippling thought process. Once again, this is a default thought process, sneaking into our minds subconsciously. Worry is the thinking of events that have not happened and are not related to the present. You think: what if my car won't start tomorrow morning, what if my roof leaks, what if I lose my money, what if they criticize me? That's worry in a nut-shell. Worry is always centered around a future event which has not taken place yet. However, since the mind is so powerful, constantly worrying about something can actually **MAKE IT COME TRUE IN THE PRESENT.** Whatever thoughts or events you constantly visualize will have a higher chance of materializing in your life.

Something happened to me as a child that I still remember to this day and can laugh about it now, but back then it was quite traumatic! When I was young, I had a whole list full of worries, a couple of them being dark places and mice. I would always be peeking under my bed multiple times before going to sleep each night. One late afternoon, my grandfather took me to a zoo-combination-park where I was allowed to ride my bike unattended. It got dark eventually, and as I was riding along near bushes looking at animals, I was worrying about the dark places where little mice could be hiding. All of a sudden, something happened on a turn I was making on the sandy ground, and I found myself landing on my rear-end right in front of a dark big bushy area. To my horror, a little mouse ran out and ran right towards me (fearlessly) as if it was going to **RUN UP MY SHORTS!** I could not believe that this unbelievable event was happening to me at the time, but I do know now that my worrying was a major cause of it transpiring. Oh, about the mouse…I quickly jumped up and I scared it away!

Here is a simple exercise to try next time you feel yourself starting to worry: **THINK OF A POSITIVE EXPERIENCE IN THE PRESENT.** Your mind cannot think of a positive and negative thought at the same time, so focus your thinking to the **PRESENT.** Worry is never a positive, life-changing experience and you must make it a priority to do your hardest to eliminate it from your thoughts as quickly as possible.

SUCCESS TIP # 25 – PERSISTENCE PAYS

There is no stronger evidence, that persistence is one of the leading factors associated with wealth creation and financial super-success. Without it you will not amount to a life above average mediocrity. No "ifs," "ands" or "buts."

A simple exercise follows to test your level of persistence.

Set your alarm clock and wake up at 5 a.m. tomorrow morning. Quickly don your tracksuit and go for an early morning jog. Do this again the following morning. Do this action **EVERY SINGLE DAY UNTIL IT TURNS INTO A HABIT.** Thirty days have gone by. Are you still accomplishing your morning jog ritual? You will be astonished to know that only 1% of the population will have the determination and pit-bull tenacity to have turned this early morning jog into a daily habit.

Believe it or not, you can actually train yourself to become more persistent. Persistence it a state of mind and quite changeable and influential. Here are a number of things that you can do to increase your persistence:

- **Mentoring.** Find a harmonious group, partner, or friend and work toward a common goal.
- **Habit.** As noted above, constant action forces the mind to accept defeat and persistence will rule.
- **Experience.** This ads the encouragement to know that your actions are correct and to keep going.

- **Solid Plans.** Plans of any kind, even unsubstantiated and unproven, are better than no plans at all.
- **Self-confidence.** This strong character trait will assist in staying on course and meeting your final outcomes.
- **Passion.** Can be described as a "white-heat" or a "feeding-frenzy." An unbelievably strong feeling associated with your goals/dreams must be present.
- **Focused Determination.** You must know what your goals/dreams are, and you must be willing to stop at nothing in achieving them.

There you are. Master the above council, and persistence will take you to the life you have always dreamed of. In effect, you will name your price and life will gladly open its wallet to pay!

SUCCESS TIP #26 – LOSE THE "WEEKEND" MENTALITY

Here is some advice that I know a lot of people are going to need a little persuading, before they actually commit themselves to putting into action. It's called losing the "weekend" mentality. What this is, is more a thought process than anything else, but it is a very unique one, as the masses have not taken the time to discover it or understand it.

Are you one of the average folks who works Monday to Friday for approximately 40 hours, where you dread Mondays with a passion and look forward to Fridays with tremendous anticipation? You earn a living for those five days and then you live your "family lifestyle" on the weekends.

The most successful individuals have integrated their work and home lives together and spread them across the full seven days and the full 168 hours in a week. As business owners, they have the flexibility of creating their own time and balance it perfectly like a circus performer in action!

Your main goal in business will be serve your customers with an outstanding product and/or service. Your customers, expecting the most incredible customer service, will want what you have to sell—and they will want it at a time that is convenient to them. This may be in the evenings, on weekends, or right before you are going to bed. If you deal with customers on the East or West Coasts, their time differences will add to the confusion. To be in business means satisfying your customers—and this means being at their beck and

*HOW TO CREATE AN UNLIMITED INCOME
SITTING AT HOME IN YOUR PAJAMAS*

call—MANY TIMES 7 DAYS A WEEK.

I can hear my readers groaning right now, "This Michael guy must be going bananas…he wants us to work 24 – 7."

You're almost right! If you are getting into this entrepreneurial game, get in to win. **IF YOU ARE NOT WILLING TO PAY THE PRICE OF SUCCESS – GET OUT OF THE GAME** (and go watch some TV). The truth of the matter is…if you are not willing to pay the price—**ONE OF YOUR COMPETITORS IS.**

Let me paint you a rosy picture now. You have followed my advice and ideas and started a business. You suddenly have a winning idea and the phones are ringing off the hook! Congratulations! You have to be ready to fill your orders and satisfy your customers; you have to run with your winners! Get help right away to fulfill your orders, even if it is the evenings or on the weekends. Keep your methods of contact open at all times, your phone, your fax, your e-mail, must all be ready and operable to do business. And be prepared for success—even if it means mending your business and family time together seven days a week. Try this new way of thinking on for size, you will find it quite liberating.

SUCCESS TIP #27 – CHANGE WILL HAPPEN ON ITS OWN

Change will happen in a split second, either by its own doing, or with your assistance. But unless you take an active approach in making changes, the only happenings taking place in your life will be crises. Change is actually crisis in disguise. Have you ever had a day when multiple setbacks have prompted you to yell: "This is the worst day of my life?" **This is a perfect example of crisis trying to make a change.**

Jump into the river of life without any direction … and you will be simply doing the dog-paddle down the rapids, at the mercy of the rocks and waterfalls up ahead! Be aware of this phenomenon and understand that it is a segment of life that cannot be avoided. To assist you in making measurable beneficial changes, you first have to know that a change is in order (you have to want it badly enough). You then must know that only YOU have full control to make the necessary changes, if you so desire. Thirdly, you must have a strong belief that CHANGE IS POSSIBLE and within your capabilities. Lastly, go ahead and take CONSISTENT ACTION to bring about the changes in your life. That's it, simple as 1, 2, 3, 4.

SUCCESS TIP #28 – BE FLEXIBLE

All prosperous individuals leave the back door open to alternate escape routes! When devising plans of any kind, careful thought should be made in advance to create multiple routes to your goal. You do not want to be banging your head against the wall, you want to be able to shift into a different course of action when you experience total resistance and overwhelming frustration.

Certain large amounts of frustration are normal in achieving immense success, but if you see yourself not making progress in reaching your goals **OVER A LONG PERIOD OF TIME AND EFFORT**, then this is an indication that you have to change paths. Your destination will still remain the same, but the journey you take will be different. Always make sure you have a "plan B" card ready to use at your discretion!

SUCCESS TIP #29 – CREATIVITY RULES

Look around you at the chair or couch you sit on, the furniture around you, the home you live in, the thousands of products you interact with….and know that all these items were thoughts in somebody's mind a long time ago! This is amazing but true. Every product or service which you use, ultimately was born from someone's mind. A creative idea!

Creativity and imagination are two very powerful forces which you should do your best in developing. Try to generate as many ideas as you can. **WRITE THEM DOWN - AND THEN PUT PLANS INTO ACTION TO DEVELOP THEM.** Many people have great ideas, but they don't cast them in stone by writing them down or take the necessary actions to create them into reality.

SUCCESS TIP #30 – POSITIVE EXPECTATIONS

Whatever expectations you place into your mind, will eventually materialize in your life. What you expect with intense dedication will eventually become your reality. Ironically, you have the power to expect **GOOD THINGS TO HAPPEN TO YOU.** It is your freedom of choice. Therefore, try to look for the good in every person or setback you experience. Try to remain self-confident, calm and expect positive outcomes. See the glass of water as half-full, not half-empty. Be an **OPPOSING-PARANOID** – Imagine that the whole world is out to **DO GOOD TO YOU**. Put this advice into daily practice, you will notice good events happening around you.

SUCCESS TIP #31 – SUCCESS AFTER 40

Countless research has aided me in revealing a very common characteristic between wealthy and successful individuals. Most of them made their most outstanding progress and success **AFTER THE AGE OF 40** and some well into their 50s and 60s. The main reason for this is that before the age of 40, most people are **UNFOCUSED AND WASTEFUL OF THEIR ENERGIES.** Think back to your life in your 20s…could you at that time have achieved outstanding success with the actions you were executing? Probably not! And now think of some of the most successful individuals of the past and know that they were past 40 when they succeeded greatly. Some examples: Ray Kroc, Colonel Sanders, and Sam Walton.

Make it habit to focus your passions, love, drive, desires, and determination to worthwhile actions which will lead you to your final outcomes. Expect a long journey, and know that it may not be for many years, deep into your 40s, when you will experience your ultimate and greatest successes.

SUCCESS TIP #32 – THE IMPORTANCE OF VALUES

We talked about values being on the same line as your goals in success tip #1. I wish to go into this topic in a little more detail now.

Values are a feeling, strong belief or conviction that is intertwined with your **ULTIMATE WELLBEING**. Your values should always be on the same plane as your goals. If they are not, you will experience a feeling of **"EMPTINESS"** after reaching your goal. You will think: "Is that all there is? There must be more to it than this!"

One example I can draw upon from my past to share with you is that in my crazy 20s, one of my main goals was to be extremely appealing to the opposite sex. I decided that I would train my body and become a male exotic dancer. After putting my plans into action and eventually reaching my goal of becoming a dancer, I found my goal competing with my values in a strong and unexpected way! I started dreading the drunk ladies throwing themselves at me, and viewing me only as a sex object. It just didn't "sit right" in my stomach, and I came to the realization that this new-found dancing position would not bring me to true fulfillment. Needless to say, I exited the profession quite abruptly, gaining knowledge about myself and my values in the process.

Other examples of goals conflicting with values: your goal of becoming a billionaire may conflict with your value of "spending more quality time with your family," your goal of being the best club bouncer may conflict with your values of being a "likeable" person (after getting into a few fights), your goal of working in a slaughterhouse may conflict with your value of a "prestigious employment position capable of producing great accomplishments."

Values are usually centered around a number of subjects which you feel strongly about. Some of these are: retirement, travel, spirituality, meaningful contribution, relationships, leisure time, friendships, possessions, wealth, security, excellent health, uncluttered mind, money, power, and success.

Make a list of your top 15 values and make sure that they match your top 15 goals. This way, you will have a better chance of leading a more fulfilling and harmonious life.

SUCCESS TIP #33 – POWER NAPPING

You are about to learn of an easy but rarely practiced strategy for combating fatigue during your waking hours. If you work hard all day long only to find yourself getting drowsy between the hours of 2 p.m. to 5 p.m., then keep reading! Taking a short power nap in the middle of the day (or as soon as you get home if you are employed outside your home) is a fantastic way to boost your efficiency. When awake for 16 to 18 hours a day, it is normal for one to start feeling tired around the middle of the day.

Countless large business have realized the importance of fighting stress at work and increasing the productivity of their employees, that they have begun adding nap tents or nap rooms, complete with alarm clocks and small cots, into their daily business practices. They encourage their employees to take power naps to invigorate them during the day and to increase the company's bottom line!

Many leaders and inventors used napping as a rule in their lives. Some of these included: Thomas Edison (took short naps in his laboratory), Abraham Lincoln and Napoleon Bonaparte. Even entire countries like Greece and Italy employ this strategy, as their residents sleep in the afternoons and all business shuts down, only to resume later on in the evening.

Take a 30 to 45 minute nap every day. Do not sleep for more than an hour, as you will fall into a deep sleep and you will have problems falling asleep later on in the evening. A short power nap will also allow you to cut one to two hours of sleep at night. So if you usually sleep eight hours a night, by napping you may be able to cut this time down to six hours. Being successful sometimes means doing the small things that others overlook. So do your best to include napping into your daily schedule and you will find yourself becoming more productive during your work hours.

SUCCESS TIP #34 – INCH BY INCH, PIECE BY PIECE

In my experiences, I have learnt that success is more a group of varied combinations rather than one complete system of how-to information. What this means is, by creatively grouping many ideas together you piece together your own success. Success is different for everyone, so how can I tell you what success will mean to you? You may not want to value success as a monetary scoreboard. Maybe extra time, or the freedom to do as you please, is success to you. This is my reasoning for packing this book with a ton of different ideas, so that you can piece the success puzzle together on your own to suit your needs and wants.

For me, earning millions of dollars per year was never a priority. I am happy to earn $2,000 - $3,000 a day, and lead a carefree lifestyle working from home, in a number of professions that are personally gratifying. For you, earning a million dollars a year may be your top priority. This may require you to work 16 hour days, seven days a week and take incredible risks in the process…are you prepared for this sacrifice? What if I could show you how to earn $3,000 a week, working only three days a week…would this be an ideal situation for you and your family? Think about it.

As you read along, you will see ideas that greatly interest you, and others which you will skim by without great enthusiasm…and that's okay. Take the systems that you think will work best for your individual situation, and mend them together to create a lifestyle which you will thrive in. Do not try to implement every single idea at once, as this will prove to be a frustrating and overwhelming task.

Please note: as you get into Part Two of my book, you must take actions in a uniform and step-by-step nature, following my instructions. Do not move on to step two unless step one is completed to perfection. Do not skip steps and go from step one to step four, as you will miss the important details in between. You can't run unless you learn how to walk first!

SUCCESS TIP #35 – BUILD CREDIT & BEAT THE BANKS

I can bet that at some point in your life you have been bombarded by credit card companies offering you free no-annual-fee cards for the chance of taking you on as a client. The card companies know that the average American or Canadian will max his/her credit card, and will have a difficult time in paying down the principal amount. In short, the banks will hold "the noose around your neck" and at the drop of a dime, execute you! You are tired of the banks always coming out ahead with their high interest charges and outrageous fees, meanwhile you end up holding the short end of the stick.

There is a way to build existing credit or establish new credit, all by using banks and **THEIR FUNDS**. It is the systematic process of using $500 or $1,000 of your own money to get the ball rolling, but then using the money from several banks to steam roll yourself into an excellent credit rating.

This is a process which I have used myself with great success, and is quite easy to do. Start by taking the above mentioned amount and placing it into a savings account at a new bank. Try going to a smaller neighbourhood bank or trust company and avoid the larger commercial banks, as the larger banks will have stringent bank rules that will make it more difficult for you to implement. If you do not have the $500 start-up amount, borrow it from friends or relatives, or use one of your credit cards. Interest rates will be of no importance, as you compare the benefits you will reap in building a superb credit rating.

Next, make an appointment with the bank manager and meet with him. Tell him that you are interested in applying for a **SECURED LOAN** using your savings account as collateral. Since this is a fairly risk-free transaction, most likely your loan will be approved. Sometimes banks are funny, and will want to only give you 50% of the value of your funds, do not agree to this, it is totally ludicrous....go out and find another bank willing to give you full face value for your secured funds. After you have received your loan funds, take the money and go to a different bank where you will repeat the process. Go through the same procedure with a minimum of 3 banks and up to 5, if time permits. Make your interest payments before the due date, this will show that you are a responsible and credit-worthy individual.

After a short while, you should be able to borrow funds with your signature alone—what is called an **UNSECURED SIGNATURE LOAN.** Start repeating the above process once again, but this time borrowing larger amounts like $2,000 or $3,000. Work this borrowing plan on a consistent and ongoing basis.

I have heard of many stories of people who have built tremendous credit lines in this fashion—some even borrowing one million dollars on their signature alone! With the process of repetition, what you are creating, in effect, is a millionaire's credit rating. The larger loan amounts will probably take years to establish, but imagine the power this will afford you. At any point, on your signature alone you will have the ability to **BEAT THE BANKS AND USE THEIR FUNDS** to build a financially secure life for yourself.

Furthermore, on the subject of banks, here is an interesting tid-bit of information. When the banks are touting their products (mutual funds, GIC's, RRSP's, savings bonds) the banks stock is actually appreciating at rates four times the returns of the products they are selling to you! Want to make more money when dealing with the banks? Purchase bank stocks, **NOT THEIR PRODUCTS.** Keep in mind, though, that you will not receive even close to wealth–building rates of returns that we discussed earlier in this chapter.

SUCCESS TIP #36 – FOLLOW YOUR PASSION

Every one of us has our own hidden talents. Deep down inside, you will know what that is. Just follow your heart. You will have your own unique circumstances, skills, experiences and knowledge, that when combined, form a complete picture of your existence. You may be a great artist, or a talented musician, or a gifted golfer. When you take the time to think it over, you will discover something that you excel in above everyone else.

Now, when creating a profession or a business as we will be learning in future chapters, do your utmost to follow your passions and somehow include them in your work. You will be laboring for long hours at the start of your company, so you don't want to be doing something you hate. Your passion is something that you would gladly do for **FREE 16 hours a day** – and you would not even notice that the time has gone by. This small tip alone will assist you in creating a fulfilling lifestyle of your choosing.

SUCCESS TIP #37 – TAKE A SOLITARY BREAK

With our growing hectic lives, kids, bills, work, family obligations...it's a wonder sometimes that we don't get an early heart attack! One way you can relieve some of this stress is by taking an uninterrupted solitary break each day. You must be completely alone, no spouses or kids allowed. Find a quiet, semi-dark place (perhaps in a bathtub or a jacuzzi) and just close your eyes and relax for a minimum of 15 to 30 minutes. Televisions and radios are also strictly forbidden.

During your break, let your mind wander over new ideas, opportunities, or ways of self-improvement. You will not believe the benefits that this little exercise offers, as far as relaxing you and generating creative thoughts. Give it a try, you will be pleasantly surprised!

SUCCESS TIP #38 – DO-IT-YOURSELF FINANCIAL MANAGEMENT

Consumer debt has reached astronomical levels in recent years. We are constantly being yelled at by advertisers: buy now pay one year down the road, or buy no-money-down, no interest, no payments for 90 days, and so on and so on. The average American family has $10,000 in consumer debt, and some have much more.

I have first-hand knowledge of what it is like fighting the losing battle of debt. Going from bankruptcy in the recession of the '90s and then building a solid financial footing gave me actual-world knowledge that I wish to pass on to you. If you are drowning in a sea of debt, pay close attention to the following words of wisdom!

- **Watch and record every penny.** For the next 30 days I would like you to record every penny that departs from your life. Whether you write it down in a notebook, or type it into your computer or day-timer, just keep track of every single penny you spend. Your income (as an employee) is probably fixed and does not change, so you don't have to spend too much thought on that.
- **Cut out the little "extras" that add up.** After doing the exercise of calculating where every penny goes, you will begin to see where all the little "extra" money leaks are. Your goal is to plug these leaks up. What are little

extras? These are petty amounts that add up considerably, and you can delete from your lifestyle without affecting you greatly. Things like: daily gourmet coffees, daily lunches out (brown bag it instead), expensive dinners out (stay home more often), massages, hair dresser appointments, manicures, waxing, satellite TV, magazine/newspaper subscriptions, cell phones, pagers, etc. It is these small expenses that are killing you financially.

- **Create a primary investment account.** As soon as you get your paycheque, pay a minimum of 10% of your gross pay into your primary investment account. Do this **before** you pay any bills, mortgages, etc. Do your best to save more than 10%...the more the merrier!
- **Make sure it's automated.** People are lazy by nature, so you don't want to have to write a cheque for your investment account every few weeks, because you will end up putting it off. Set it up as an automated withdrawal plan right from your account on the day you normally get paid.
- **Pay double the minimum payment on credit cards.** If you are making only the minimum payment on your credit cards, you will be leaving this debt to your beneficiaries! Pay twice what your minimum payment is, and you will start lowering your principal amount this way. If you can put more than double the payment, go right ahead.
- **If you own a home (and I hope you do) change your mortgage payment to a weekly or bi-weekly one.** Since there are 52 weeks in a year, you will end up making one extra payment each year. This will shave approximately 7 years off your mortgage, and save you thousands of dollars in the process. Did you know that if you purchased a $100,000 home and carried it over 30 years at around 10% interest rate, you would have dished out an unbelievable $300,000 (three times the value of the home)! Now this is definitely not smart. Once again, the banks don't tell you these things, so that they can keep profiting from your ignorance.
- **Save your money.** Following are a few great ways to come out ahead financially:

>Don't buy new, always buy things used (especially vehicles).
>Pay cash whenever you can, never lease or finance.
>Become a do-it-yourselfer around your home and on your car.
>Purchase the best quality items you can afford, and wear them out.
>Shop for bargains and use coupons.
>Don't be an impulse buyer—why do you think the candy/gum is by the cash registers?

Plan to buy in advance—if you need a winter coat, buy it in the summer for 1/3 the price.
Stay healthy, pay less in medicine and doctors bills.
Guard what you have and practice routine maintenance to increase the life of the product.
Increase deductibles on home and auto insurance—this lowers payments.
Bargain at every possibility when dealing with stores.
Never buy service–extended warranties, they are rarely worth it.
Buy generic…not name brands.
Buy a used bike as an alternate mode of transportation.
Get rid of collision insurance on older vehicles.
Install alarms and anti-theft devices–they lower insurance rates.
Plan ahead and pay with cash–not instant-bank cards or credit cards.
If the government owes you a refund, do your taxes early, they don't pay interest.
Pay down your mortgage by making extra principle payments whenever you can.
Rent a video or DVD instead of going to the movies.
Marry rich.
Give the undertaker a rubber check.

- **Cut up all your consumer credit cards.** Get out from under this debt albatross for once and for all!

SUCCESS TIP #39 – PROTECT YOURSELF

It is a known fact that we are living longer and longer each year. Take care of yourself every day, and you might live to be eighty or ninety. That is why it is extremely important to make sure that you are adequately insured. You are more likely to suffer an accident or disability in your lifetime than you are of dying at an unexpectedly early age. It is a wise decision to purchase **disability insurance** to cover any temporary loss of income. This insurance is quite affordable, around $100 per month, and well worth the investment. Make sure that it is renewable and non-cancelable. Make sure your policy includes a rider to cover the costs of inflation. As a future entrepreneur, this is the first insurance to purchase on your to-do list!

If you have a large family with dependants, it will be wise to also take out

term life insurance to protect against any complete loss of income. If you are a bachelor, or have a working spouse with a high income (and no dependants), then getting this type of insurance will not be that important.

Putting your insurance needs in place sometimes requires thinking of the worst case scenarios. One of these is a terminal or crippling illness or injury where the patient cannot think for himself. A **living will** can assist with this difficult situation. A competent attorney can advise you as far as the items which will need to be included.

Finally, make sure to get a lawyer to also prepare a **will** for you, as you never know when you will die. You should include a letter of instruction detailing how you wish your assets to be shared. One area which should not be overlooked is items of sentimental value or other heirlooms. Such items are always of major importance to remaining family members and usually result in vicious disagreements.

SUCCESS TIP #40 – SOME REAL ADVICE ON REAL ESTATE

Real estate is an arena that I have a large background of experience in. I have been an avid reader as well as purchaser of personal and investment property for many years now. One of my businesses (for the past five years now) is an advertising and marketing agency specializing in new home builders and developers. My strategic marketing campaigns and cutting-edge creative materials have assisted my clients in **selling millions of dollars worth of property year over year.**

Real estate is one of the largest and most important investments you will probably make in your lifetime, and you should take your time to research and study this excellent wealth-building vehicle very carefully. I will give you some practical pointers in this section. I will not dig deep into the details, as there are many books on the subject that specialize in the how-to aspects of purchasing and managing real estate. You will find this section a little lengthy, but crammed with many important tips.

I am going to start off by highlighting the no-money-down gurus—you know who they are, I won't mention any names. They are a hard sell group, of mostly American background, selling courses, books, videos, tapes and expensive seminars (I will hereafter refer to them as "gurus"). They play on your emotional heartstrings, telling you that it is possible to leverage yourself into millions, all on borrowed debt and "other people's money." I'm not saying it is impossible to buy with no-money-down, as I have done it myself a number of times, however, there are certain areas that the gurus skip, or simply skim past. These are the areas that you have to watch your step on, so here are a few of them:

- **Market conditions.** Real estate has its ups and downs. Real estate cycles last approximately seven years. When it is a seller's market, there are few properties on the market and buyers bid fast to pick up what is left, many times bidding against each other and going over the listed price. I dare you during these times to try and find a vendor who will accept a no-money-down offer. They will be non-existent! So therefore, realize that these deals do not and will not happen in every market condition. When listings are rare, and prices are strong, vendors will never accept no-money-down deals.
- **Renters market.** Many of the guru's strategies involve buying properties, and then finding tenants to cover all the expenses. What they lack to inform you of though, is that when interest rates are extremely low (as they are now) many renters can afford to buy their own homes, and many of them do. That is when it becomes extremely difficult to find tenants to put into your properties. Many landlords have to lower rents to attract tenants and it becomes increasingly difficult this way to have a positive cash flow on your property. Many apartments which were renting for $1,000 are now renting for $600…it is truly a renters market! It is wise to place a test ad to rent a property BEFORE YOU ACTUALLY BUY IT…just to check what the renters market is like in your area. If you can't find a tenant, you will have to make the extra mortgage payment and expenses out of your own pocket…and this can be financially draining.
- **Regional prices.** Understand that no-money-down deals do not work in all areas of the country. The gurus might tell you that it is possible, but don't you believe it. Many areas with high-priced real estate like California, Toronto, and Vancouver will have such expensive properties, that it is a near impossibility to buy with no down payment and rent the property out at a break even or positive cash flow. Additionally, there are areas where vendors are not selling for no-money-down. Just open your local newspaper and try to find a for sale by owner who is advertising a vendor take back mortgage. I bet you will not find one. I bet if you searched for a whole year, you would still not find one!
- **Closing costs.** Most of the gurus do not discuss the closing costs involved

with purchasing property or skim by it at lightning speed. There are large expenditures required up front, things like: lawyers' fees, disbursements, loan applications, brokers' fees, insurance fees and land transfer taxes. Many vendors and real estate agents will not pay for these costs, no matter how well of a negotiator you are. There is also the cost of high ratio mortgages which is never discussed.

- **Maintenance and repairs.** I don't care how diligent you are in selecting your property, there will always be unforeseen maintenance and repairs with every property you purchase. It is Murphy's law, if something can go wrong, it will. The roof will need replacing, the foundation will leak, or the furnace will quit on you. During your ownership of your property, something unforeseen will surely happen, and this will take a $2,000 to $5,000 bite (and sometimes more) from your expected profits. Many times the maintenance costs alone will cause you to have a negative cash flow. Be extra careful when purchasing properties that are about 22 years old, as many items on these homes will have reached their useful age and will need replacing. Items such as windows/doors, skylights, roofs, furnaces, air conditioning units, central vacuums, wood decks/balconies, will require major repairs or replacement.
- **Source of excellent monthly income**. This is probably the biggest myth of the gurus selling points. They tell you that real estate is an excellent cash generator providing positive cash flow on a monthly basis. This is a bunch of baloney! Any experienced real-world investor will tell you that just one month of vacancy, one unforeseen maintenance problem, one tenant problem, can wipe out your entire yearly expected profits! There is such a small margin of error when purchasing no-money-down real estate that any small emergency (and trust me it will happen) will destroy your positive cash flow expectations!
- **Dealing with tenants is a nightmare.** Face it, a tenant will have little respect for, and will not care as much for your asset as you will. The gurus never concentrate on this major point. Here is the reality and no fluff on tenants: Tenants are transient by nature and you will have to contend with turnover. When a tenant moves out, you will have to clean, paint, advertise and show the property to new tenants—this takes a lot of time and money. Tenants are younger than owners, with lower incomes and jobs that are not established, so finding good tenants is extremely difficult. If they had great jobs and excellent credit they would be buying their own homes, now wouldn't they? And if you do get lucky and find a fantastic tenant, they will not stay for long, as they will be saving to buy their own home in the near future.

When ever the phone rings and it is one of your tenants, from my experience, it is never good news! The problems are always major when dealing with tenants. I remember awakening in the early morning due to the fire alarms going off in one of my rooming houses. To my horror, I found a tenant fast asleep with a two-foot-round fire in the middle of her room. An exotic dancer by trade, she had come home late, intoxicated, and had fallen asleep with her cigarette burning in her purse! Another time, one of my tenants got laid off, and so he decided to start a drug–dealing operation from his room. Needless to say, this attracted a lot of other low class individuals to my property, who in turn ended up causing other damages and disturbances. I quickly terminated this tenant's rental contract due to legal grounds—I squealed, and the cops raided his room and arrested him!

Other considerations are rent controls and the disturbing circumstances this has on landlords. Many states and provinces have landlord-tenant laws that favor the tenant and so it is very costly and a time burden to evict a tenant. Sometimes it is impossible to evict a tenant in the middle of winter. These rules and regulations make the purchase of rental property very unfavorable, since having control is high on our priority list (as discussed earlier). When you play by somebody else's rules, they control your life and you are powerless to change this.

When looking for tenants, do not rent to the first smiling face that comes to your door. Scrutinize and take your time. Always have tenants fill out an application, rental contract, and a move in/out form. Check references carefully, do a credit check, and phone their place of employment. Take extra care in contacting previous landlords other than the one where they are leaving from, as current landlords may have something nice to say just to get rid of their "loser" tenant. Also watch out for these warning flags:

Someone who refuses to fill out an application
No bank account or checking account
No established job or claims of self-employment with a big income
Tenants who try to lower your asking price (never negotiate with a tenant)
Has no landlord references
Someone without proper identification
Tenants who want to pay the deposit by using installments
Families too big for the unit you are renting
Tenants with large pets that do big damage

- **Not a home-based business.** The acquisition process, the renovating process, the renting process, the maintenance process, all require the owner to make countless drives out of their home. The gurus stress this great home-based opportunity, when in fact there are countless driving excursions required to find a property, rent it and maintain it. They blindly argue that a "management company" can do this for you, but these companies charge fees (around 10%) which eat away at your profits and create negative cash flows. Some gurus want you to hire a managing partner, but you cannot really do this unless you have a number of properties under your belt and you know what you are doing.

- **Other myths and truths.** The gurus tell the unknowing first-time buyers to take on hundreds of thousands of dollars worth of debt and put their credit on the line. Beginning investors just don't have the knowledge to go into such risky ventures and come out winners. The gurus never stress the risks involved: Trying to sell in a down market. Treating real estate as a short-term speculative investment. Trying to find good tenants. Buying property in a regional market with one large employer – and that employer goes bankrupt. There are countless factors that can affect the outcome of real estate and these are always ignored. In fact, one can question if the gurus are doing so well by buying and selling real estate, then how come they are doing the hotel rounds…selling expensive courses and direct marketing kits?

Listen to me when I tell it to you like it is. It is possible to buy for no-money-down, but do it cautiously. Do some careful study of real estate, and do it on your own (not with no-money-down courses), and then buy with sound investment practices.

Many fortunes are based around real estate, just open a *Forbes* magazine and you will see a large percentage of the wealthiest individuals with strong bases in ownership of land. Ted Turner is supposedly the largest land-owner in the United States. Arnold Schwartzenegger began his rise to wealth by investing in real estate. Land is limited, they are not making more of it. So buy it. Buy it and wait. Over time, real estate will always appreciate even as it goes through its ups and downs, but eventually it will always come back up. This is a historic fact that cannot be ignored. If the purchase of one principal residence can have such an enormous outcome to your financial future, imagine what could happen if you buy just one other property, or two, or three?

I do not give you any fairytale gospel, just common-sense practical advice. Here are some more words of wisdom to assist you, if you decide to use real estate to supplement your wealth goals.

- **Always have a licensed inspector** check out a prospective property, paying close attention to the foundation and other major defects, as well as future deferred maintenance issues.
- **Take your time** and shop around cautiously. Do not let a salesperson force you to make a sale before you are satisfied that you have found the perfect property.
- **Have the property appraised** before you buy it. You make your profit when you buy, not when you sell. Look for the worst looking property in the best neighbourhood.
- **Do business only with licensed** and experienced real estate agents. Check out their reputations by calling on their references. Use an agent that you feel comfortable with and has an understanding for the type of property you are purchasing. If you are looking for investment property, use an agent who owns investment property of their own.
- **Buyer beware.** You will be putting your credit report on the line, and tying up funds for a very long time (as real estate is not a liquid asset). Go over all paper work, think of all possible circumstances which could go wrong, check and double check, before signing your signature. There are many reasons why a vendor will withhold pertinent information concerning a property. Case in point: I recently purchased a property, which I found out later from a neighbour had been used by a previous tenant as a marijuana grow house!
- **Know the real estate market and be aware of other factors.** Study carefully and watch the news. The best deals are bought at the bottom of the real estate cycle. Always know that rises and falls in pricing are only temporary. The end of one cycle means the beginning of another one. As long as you are able to wait, eventually you will always make money. Be aware, too, that sometimes events such as illness, a death, divorce, job transfer, job loss, can force you to sell at a loss. Other factors will have an affect on the value of real estate such as: employment conditions, economic climate, location of the property, population trends, rental vacancy rates, traffic flow, crime and proximity of shopping amenities. As a potential future investor, have you given these factors any thought?
- **Always use an experienced real estate lawyer** to handle the transaction. Make sure you insure the title of the property, this is also paramount.
- **Real estate is a long-term proposition.** If you jump in and out of the market, the real estate commissions and taxes will take their share of your

profits. Plus, you may be at the bottom of the real estate cycle and lose a bundle. You have to give real estate a chance to become "seasoned," to build equity. This may mean holding onto real estate for 10 years or longer. Never think of speculating or short-term, unless you enjoy giving away the "shirt on your back."

SUCCESS TIP #41 – ALL ABOUT FAILURE

Failure is an entrepreneur's companion. Like a shadow, it is always close by. But what is it really? The reality of failure is that it actually is nonexistent. **FAILURE CAN BE DESCRIBED AS ACHIEVING OR NOT ACHIEVING A GOAL.** That is all. It means we made an assumption that was incorrect, or put a plan into action that was unrealistic. In the process we discovered a set of actions that did not work. And it is up to us to learn from our mistakes and make the necessary corrections in the future.

I'm sure you are aware of this, but most of the successful people in the world went through countless obstacles, frustrations, rejections, bankruptcies, and disappointments prior to reaching the peak of the success mountain. Being an entrepreneur means jumping off a cliff and learning how to fly on the way down. Burning your bridges, and therefore making retreat an impossibility. When you take such risks, you are bound to have a few frustrations along the way. But don't worry, because colossal obstacles are a clear sign that you are on the right road to success. It means that you are not settling for mediocrity and that you are stretching yourself to do better. Just remember to be flexible in your plans, and always try to learn something from the roadblocks that you encounter.

SUCCESS TIP #42 – THE LONG JOURNEY AHEAD & HOW TO RETIRE IN FIVE YEARS

You've probably pondered how your life will turn out 10 years or 20 years from today. And you've wondered: where am I going, and how am I going to get there? I believe that one of the ways to attain inner contentment is to consider our lives as one amazing journey to experience. There will be many ups and downs on this quest, and I'm sure you have been through a few already. Mentally prepare yourself for this long journey. Realize that with the advancement of nutrition and medicine, it is a realistic possibility that you will reach the wise old age of 80!

Understand, too, that times have changed from generations ago. Backbreaking menial labor jobs are a thing of the past. This is the dawn of the information age. In this age, the most difficult tasks you will be involved in will probably be picking up the phone receiver, stuffing envelopes or typing the keys on your computer. So you can, and probably will, have to live the entrepreneur lifestyle for a very long while. As an entrepreneur you will be alone "flying like a solitary eagle in the sky of the unknown."

In the 20th century, single–income households are a thing of the past. It takes dual incomes, and sometimes clever additional income sources, to sustain our lifestyles. Get rid of the burden of trying to retire at the golden age of 65. Retiring at that age may actually be an impossibility for most people. Get into the mindset of following your lifelong passions. Of understanding that many who retire early are left with a feeling of emptiness, of excess leisure and unimportance. I'm sure you've heard of the stories of people slaving away at difficult jobs they hated all their lives, and shortly after retirement, they pass away or become seriously ill. This is why the finish line of early retirement should be erased from our minds. We must replace these thoughts with the empowering idea that the only finish line is when we take our last breath of life.

For those of you that cannot be persuaded into this new way of thinking, I ask you to embark on an alternative idea…and that is a quick five-year retirement plan! This plan will give you the freedom to pursue your passions at an age that you will be able to truly enjoy them. So forget about RRSP's, 401K's, or company pension plans. Let me offer you the following closely guarded investment advice to assist you in a speedy retirement:

- **Don't buy a house with a mortgage balance more than two times your gross yearly income.** Why? Simply because the banks readily offer you a mortgage at around 30 – 35% your income, it doesn't mean it is the proper thing to do. If you earn $100K per year you shouldn't purchase a house with a remaining mortgage of more than $200K. You don't want to over-extend yourself, finding yourself in a "ball & chain" situation working to pay off the bank for 25 years!
- **Don't purchase/lease a vehicle with a price tag more than 25% your gross yearly income.** Same as above, you don't want to dig a deep grave for yourself. A vehicle is simply meant to take you from point A to point B. Period. You really don't need a Ferrari to accomplish this. If you are like most people,

you will not be in a financial position to pay cash for the vehicle, so you will have the whole outstanding price hanging over your head.
- **Start two or three small, home-based businesses and make it a goal for yourself to double your yearly income** from what it is today. This may take you one or two years to accomplish, but after completing my book you will have hundreds of cutting-edge techniques and ideas that will assist you in accomplishing this goal.
- **Sacrifice and work hard like no other person is prepared to work** (14 – 18 hour days)…and you will later have the life that not too many other people will have….(at the age of 40 to boot)! **Do whatever it takes to double your income and pay off your mortgage and car (the 2 largest expenses in your monthly budget) within 5 years!**
- **Set up your small businesses so that they run automatically (automation-perfected: more on this in later chapters).** Your goal here is to work one to two hours each day running small businesses that you are passionate about - for the long term! What makes retirement and financial independence possible is simply this: **having a higher income coming in (automatically) than you do expenses going out.** So even if you do retire, there will always be certain costs that will never disappear, things like: food, property taxes, car insurance, toiletries, telephone bill, utility bills. You might still have monthly costs of $1,000 for example, but with your automated businesses you may be able to bring in $3,000 (quite easily) each month. This, my friends, is retirement and reaching financial freedom at a young age!

So dear readers, I advise you to look far into the future and think of this journey called life as an eye-popping extended vacation. So our voyage begins…hang onto opportunity, as she leads you into the nuts-and-bolts of creating and running a highly successful direct–marketing business, in your pajamas of course!

Part 2

Chapter 2
The Wonderful World of Direct Marketing

What is direct marketing you ask? It is a method of unsolicited advertising, targeted directly to the customer (with no middle-men) and converting them to buy your product or service, and then reselling to them again in the near future. One of the many unique features of direct marketing is that it creates an immediate, scientifically measurable response from your leads. Direct marketing can be selectively laser-focused to a specific market segment, on a small budget to test the effectiveness of your product or service. If your product/service is sound and produces a profit (all done with accurate testing), all you have to do next is rollout into larger advertising campaigns.

Direct Marketing (or direct response marketing) has five distinct categories: Direct mail, magazines, newspapers, radio and television. I am an expert in the first three categories (as they are the least expensive to advertise in), and these are probably the categories that will interest the largest group of my readers. There are also other unique methods of marketing which I will discuss later, like e-mailing, the internet, faxing and more.

What are some of the key advantages of a Direct Marketing business? Here are the most common:

- **Home-based.** You can start from your kitchen table or from a spare corner in your bedroom. There is no need for large commercial leases. Stay-at-home moms can work and still be with their children. Two-hour commutes into busy downtown cores will be a thing of the past. You will be able to work

in a carefree and stress-free environment, in your pajamas if you wish!
- **Mobility.** Face-to-face sales contact is not a requirement in this business. Therefore, you can pick up and move to any location and create the lifestyle you desire! Move to the country. Move to Florida. Move by the ocean. All you really need is an address to pick up your checks from!
- **No employees required.** I will be showing you ways to eliminate the use of employees, or at best keep their requirements to the bare minimum. A family of two adults and one assistant can do $1,000,000 worth of business revenue a year.
- **No inventory.** There are ways (like getting into the information products business) which do not require up-front inventory. And obviously, service or idea businesses do not require any inventory at all.
- **No special education, intellect or equipment/tools required.** You don't need a college, or university degree to get started. You don't need a specialized license. You don't need a genius 160 IQ....an average 100 IQ should suffice. The strategies in my book are easy to understand, even for a high school dropout. The only prerequisites are probably a fixed address, mail service, a phone line and a used personal computer.
- **Minimal up-front investment.** Unlike franchises or other business opportunities that require investments of $100,000 or more, this direct marketing system can be implemented with a few hundred dollars start-up money.
- **Low overhead.** As mentioned above, you will not need: leasing of rental space, paying employees, large equipment or machinery, purchasing large inventory....all making for one of the lowest overhead businesses around.
- **Low risks—astronomical profit potential.** The techniques I show you will be low risk. Simple "test" ads will eliminate products or services that will not work, and identify to you which ones will work. Earning $20,000 per month is a conservative income goal in this business, and I will show you how to accomplish this.
- **Automation perfected.** This business is ideal for setting up to run automatically, on it's own, with little requirement for the creator of the business to bust his behind working on a daily basis. Basically you can make money while you're sleeping. Does this idea entice you?

Furthermore, did you know that the direct response business is one of the fastest-growing businesses in America today? It is an over 30 billion-dollar-a-

HOW TO CREATE AN UNLIMITED INCOME
SITTING AT HOME IN YOUR PAJAMAS

year business with incredible global possibilities. And home-based is the way to go. There are over 25 million Americans running business out of their homes. Half of these business are service oriented. Twenty percent of U.S. home entrepreneurs reported yearly incomes of between $100,000 and $500,000 recently, while fourteen percent of them paid themselves annual salaries of $50,000 to $250,000.

Worried about job security? 1500 jobs are eliminated every day in the US, while home-based businesses continue to grow at a dramatic rate. In fact, only 5% of home-based business fail every year—this means that they enjoy a 95% survival rate. And are you looking for the security of a Fortune 500 company? In the last 15 years, Fortune 500 companies laid off nearly 10 million workers!

It just cannot be refuted, that working from a home-based direct marketing business is one of the best businesses to get into today. You can start with a few hundred dollars investment and multiply this into a $2,000/day income. Don't believe me yet? I can mention just a few extremely successful businesses that got their head start in direct response: Victoria's Secret, Dell Computers, The Sharper Image, Sears, Columbia House, Nordic Track and Lands End. Other businesses include direct response into their core business marketing strategies: companies like Avon, Amway, and AOL. There are thousands of smaller unknown mail order businesses racking in big profits on a yearly basis. Are you ready to join this successful and booming group? If you are, read on!

What I would like to reveal to you now is that the core systems of Direct Marketing can be broken down into these four step-by-step actions:

1. Find a market that requires a solution, which can be solved by creating a product, service, idea or system.

2. Create a compelling, irresistible offer or advertisement and test it with a small advertising budget.

3. Show a profit. Organize the business on a solid footing before proceeding.

4. Expand into larger advertising campaigns, and different market segments/areas.

You have to follow each step carefully and systematically, and no cheating by skipping steps. This is unmistakable…so please take note: **skipping one of the above steps can be financially devastating!** Do not even try it. But don't worry, I will take you by the hand and lead you through the complexities of each step, one at a time and in a thorough manner. If something is not clear as we go along, I advise you to go back and reread the section before deciding to put the strategies into action. So let's not waste any more time, let's get started!

FINDING OR CREATING UNIQUE PRODUCTS AND SERVICES

Your first step in direct marketing is to create, copy, or find a:
PRODUCT
SERVICE
IDEA
SYSTEM
COMBINATION OF ALL OF THE ABOVE

Following is a sentence which is worth 1000 times the cost you shelled out for the price of this book. Here it is:
MOLD YOUR IDEA TO FIT A MARKET, NOT A MARKET TO YOUR IDEA.

Need an explanation? First research to find a market that needs a product or service AND THEN create a business or idea to fill that need. In essence you have to:

Find an itch and then scratch it!

The above statements are paramount to your success in the direct marketing field. If you believe that you will create an amazing new product and service and that the whole world will beat a path to your door to acquire it…then you are sadly mistaken! It is extremely difficult and risky to do it this way. Imagine spending thousands of dollars and two whole years of time and energy to create a product and bring it to fruition, only to find that nobody wants or needs your creation? Think of the money and time which could have been saved by first seeking a market that has a need and then solving that need on a small budget. So first take the time to seriously think of a problem that needs solving. A worry that bothers the masses, which is easily fixable. Your product or service must also solve the problem quickly and easily. People want what they want, and they want it in an instant without having to wait. Surprisingly, most people make their buying decisions because of emotions…they are truly impulse-buyers!

Following are a number of unique ways to get your creative juices flowing so that you can come up with your own million-dollar idea!

START OFF WITH SATISFYING ONE OF THE BASIC HUMAN DESIRES:

Love & Sex. How-to books on picking up beautiful mates. Introduction services. Internet dating services. Pheromones for attracting the opposite sex. Enlargement devices for men. Sexual aids. Premature ejaculation problem solver. Mail-order brides. Erectile dysfunction pills or potions.

Attractiveness. Get toned and stay lean. Stay slimmer. Diet aids and weigh-loss programs are huge. Abdominal machines (how many of these infomercials have you seen lately on TV?) Any exercise equipment. Make more friends. Be more comfortable and easy to get along with. Wrinkle-free creams. Have more hair, thicker hair. Cosmetics.

Health and vitality. Ways to live longer and stay healthier. Seniors health ideas are real winners. Live stress-free. Vitamin sales. Herbal aids. Medical aids, products and services. Feel-good products. Pain relievers of any kind.

Self-improvement. Having self-confidence. Increasing memory. Destroying fear or worry. Be a better spouse or parent. Quit smoking aids.

Becoming successful. Becoming recognized. Becoming famous. Gaining power. Stand out from the crowd. Gain respect and be appreciated.

More time. Help people save time. Bring services to their homes on their terms. Mobile oil change. Landscaping. Home improvement. Help people work less. Show people how to have more leisure time. Gardening products that save time. Kitchen products that save time.

Becoming rich. Have tons of money and time freedom too. Creating wealth. Making millions. Assisting financial independence. Helping people retire quickly with more money. Getting out of debt. Saving more money.

Sell business opportunities. Being self-employed. Working from home. Starting a new profession. Starting a service business. Create a business-in-a-kit.

THE MOST CREATIVE WAYS TO ESTABLISH PRODUCTS AND SERVICES

Watch the news, cut magazine and newspaper articles. Crisis surrounds us on a daily basis. Being aware of these crisis will help you start "brainstorming" on ways to solve these concerns. The bigger the issue, the larger the profit potential. Clipping newspaper articles is a unique way of spotting trends and following patterns. If you keep seeing the same headlines and the same topics reappearing on a consistent basis, you may discover a "hot" and upcoming trend that you can capitalize on.

Think crime, violence and security. Terrorism, gangs, illegal drugs, rising crime, as well as other destructive issues has caused our society to long for safety and security. People are becoming more family-oriented and spending a considerable amount of time at home where they feel a great amount of safety and security. Any product or business based around the family home is a fantastic area to focus on. Here are some ideas: Home security, home renovations, guard dogs, home entertainment systems, home office furniture, guns, protection devises, home surveillance, child safety products.

Problems and solutions. You may have heard of the saying that every problem has a solution dragging behind it. If you can think of a large problem that you can fix with your product or service, then you probably have a winning direct marketing idea. Could it be a problem of: pollution, dangerous drivers, AIDS, cancer, high cost of real estate, leaking taps, lost contact lenses, etc. etc. The problem can be anything your heart desires. Think of some of your talents and passions and try to correlate a problem which you can solve by using the skills unique to you.

HOW TO CREATE AN UNLIMITED INCOME SITTING AT HOME IN YOUR PAJAMAS

Import a product or business. Have you ever taken a vacation or a trip to another state, province, or city and you discovered a product or service which didn't exist in your neck of the woods? This is a very powerful idea. Many people go about their trips blind to their surroundings, where in fact there are thousands of business ideas surrounding them. Next time you take a trip far from your home, have a pad and pen with you and jot down any interesting businesses or products which do not exist in your area. Or take a trip with this specific purpose in mind....to bring something of real value back with you! If a trip is not in your budget at the moment, you may want to look through import/export publications from the orient. Places like China, Taiwan and Hong Kong have thousands of possible products which a successful marketer can promote in his/her country. Try if you can to arrange for an exclusive arrangement, as they will usually try to sell to everyone they come in contact with.

Be a copy-cat. Here is one thing most people do not think about. With a new product or service, or a business which has not matured yet, there is an open playing field for any and all competitors to play their own games and write their own rules! If you see a product or service which you think is unique, and fairly new and unknown, model your own business around it. A small caution here: you must modify your idea just enough so as not to infringe on the other party's intellectual or patent rights. The marketing territory will probably be wide open for the taking. You will probably have to work at breakneck speeds to attack your competitor's market share. One thing you should be aware of is that many business segments have such growth potential that a number of competitors can all get into the game and make a good killing.

One way to find out if a business or product is successful is to pick up back issues of the magazine where the business/product appears. If you see the same ad running over the span of many months or years, you have a pretty positive atmosphere for a business that is in demand. Why would the owners of the business keep running ads if their product or service was not selling?

Change it with a few twists. It is incredibly difficult to create a unique idea, and bring it to market successfully. Thousands of dollars and endless amounts of time are involved. Of course you have exclusivity when you are finished, but it is so much easier to take something existing and modify it to add your own special touch. Many successful individuals practiced this exact idea over and over again to create some of our society's most valued products and services. Similarly, large companies copy each other on a daily basis. It is actually quite simple. Here are some ideas to get you going: make it quicker, produce the product cheaper, increase the quality, group products and services together, take ideas from one business and move them to another business category, modernize it by taking it global or on the internet, change the price (up/down).

Place a classified ad in the newspaper. Yes you heard me right. Place an ad to attract manufacturers or inventors to send you their information. Make sure that you have a release form so that they understand that you will not steal their ideas. You will be surprised to see the amount of replies which you will receive from your $30 ad. It's a known fact that about 95% of patents never make it to the market place. The inventors never took the extra steps required to market their ideas. Since you will have the necessary knowledge after reading my material, you will be able to work out a satisfactory royalty system with the inventor to use his idea for mutual profit.

Search the directories. There are a number of very useful directories which you can use to find manufacturers or wholesalers for a new product. You can also use the directories for creative brainstorming to come up with new ideas. They can be viewed at your public library or you can do a search on the internet and try to find them there. Here is a listing of the most common business directories to start your search in:
THOMAS DIRECTORY
GALE DIRECTORIES
WARD'S BUSINESS DIRECTORY
AMERICAN WHOLESALERS AND DISTRIBUTORS DIRECTORY

Find a business that needs "completing." In any given market place there are businesses that exist, but do not truly fulfill all the complete needs of their customers. Customers today are bombarded with competition wherever they turn, but many times are not getting their full needs fulfilled. If you can spot a business segment which you can "tailor more completely" to fit the needs of their customers, then you will have another great idea in the making. Look into this further.

Create and manufacture your own product. A creative product is perfect for the person who is adventurous and wants exclusivity of his creation, as well as full control over the manufacturing process. A well thought of and ingenious product can generate a nice little income for you. I have personally made over $15,000 a month in the past by creating and manufacturing just one product. Many times I market multiple products and services at the same time to generate the most income I can. With a little practice, I am pretty confident that you can do the same!

Again, start off with an area that you have a passion about and then do some research on the world wide web or at the nearest library. Make sure that your product satisfies one of the human desires mentioned earlier.

There are many manufacturing methods available to create your own creative product. Plastic, rubber, wood, ceramics, lead, glass (not recommended), fiberglass, cloth, steel and aluminum are all excellent materials to use. Be extra careful that the product you are creating is not too large, or too heavy, as this will add to the shipping costs later on. This idea is suitable for people who are "handy" and can build unique products. I remember hearing about a couple who was making a fortune selling clothes for pets through the mail!

Many creative and intellectual products are so unique that they must be patented. I won't get into the legalities of getting a product patent, but I advise you to do so if you find you have an exceptional demand for your product. If you don't patent, you run the obvious risk of someone stealing your idea. "Reverse Engineering" is the re-constructing of your product or idea piece by piece, for copying purposes. Most manufactured products can be taken apart very easily and "reverse engineered." The opposite is seen in a trade secret of a food or soft drink—do you know the exact ingredients in: your favorite soft drink, the secret sauce on your favorite fast food burger, or the delicious coating on your favorite fast food fried chicken? I don't think so. These are well-guarded trade secrets!

One funny thing about creating and manufacturing your own product is that you will get many offers from people who are interested in purchasing your product to retail themselves. I do this periodically when I am sure to receive a large order, and am completely satisfied that my products will not be marketed in a way that is obviously in direct competition with my own marketing system. I also make sure that when wholesaling to others, I allow for a healthy markup (not full retail markup) but enough to make a good profit. We will be talking about pricing your products and services shortly.

Keep in mind that one of the biggest benefits of a product that you build is that you do not have to carry large amounts of inventory. You are basically **"manufacturing upon demand."** You receive an order first and then you build your product after, therefore eliminating any risks or high cash investments up-front. You don't run the risk of having a basement full of unwanted products that don't sell! Also note that you will probably require certain materials suppliers to create your product, and these suppliers will do their best in coercing you to purchase their materials in bulk (to save you money). I always advise you to buy in the smallest amounts at the beginning "test" phase of a new idea, to again keep your financial outlay to a minimum.

One disadvantage of creating a product that you manufacture is the constant extra time and labor involved every time your products are purchased and you have to build new ones. So not only do you have the initial research and development (which may take years), but then when you bring your product to market and it is a success, you have to put the manufacturing processes in place to make sure you meet the demand. Of course, building products in-house, you can keep a close watch on quality control to make sure your products do not leave your business in a defective manner. And then you get into the dilemma of requiring employees to build your products, and the zoning issues of having a manufacturing plant in a residential location. Please think of all these issues carefully. You do not want to be trapped in your dark basement, gluing and welding widgets 20 hours a day, because you have a hot product on your hands and don't want to deal with employees or zoning inspectors!

One key benefit of going the creative product route? **Complete exclusivity and control. Owning a business or idea, or having full control over one, is clearly the quickest path to financial super-stardom.**

Nobody can come by and "pull the rug out from under your feet." Nothing beats this feeling of total control over your future destiny!

Drill your friends and relatives. Many of your acquaintances will have great ideas inside of them and no way of making them a reality. With a little coaxing, by asking them to assist you in developing your own business, many will be more than happy to reveal to you some knowledge, idea, or product which they have kept on the back-burner. Your goal here is to ask in a non-threatening way, almost as if you are asking for their help and advice. I will throw a caution to the wind here: unless it is an extremely guarded product which they will want a share of the profits, do not even for a minute think of taking on a relative as a business associate. You do not need them. Direct marketing is such a low overhead business, that you can self-finance it yourself without the need of partners. I would strongly argue against making a family member an active partner in your business (trust me, I have experience in this area). Think about it. Will you be able to fire Uncle Harry if the business goes sour or if he doesn't follow through with his part of the agreement? Keep business and personal relationships separate.

So perhaps Uncle Harry knows of a magical ingredient for a face cream which destroys acne. Great! I would give him a small piece of the pie from every sale you make rather than making him an active partner. Create a royalty system and put it into place. Uncle Harry will be happy to receive a royalty check every month, without having to work for it!

Study the boomers. The biggest group of the population which was born from 1946 through to 1964 is going to be an explosive industry in the near future. Their spending power will be increasing as they get older so they will have a larger voice in our marketing programs. A business or product that assists seniors in any of the following categories is sure to be an excellent income-earner with strong and steady growth potential:

Investments, financing and retirement.
Health care or home health care
Housing (bungalows and condos)
Leisure and recreation
Wellbeing and vitality
Home renovation

The immigrants are coming. One big demographic change that has been going on for the past while, and will continue to do so in the years to come, is the new cultural and immigration growth in North America. Serving these newly arrived immigrants with products or services tailored specifically at them will most surely be a profitable niche area. So the immigrants are coming…search for ways to: house them, educate them, feed them, keep them healthy, make them wealthy, and offer them leisure activities. Getting any ideas?

Reincarnate an old product. If you've ever opened up very old magazines or catalogues, you will be blown away by some of the fantastic products that were marketed 40 or 50 years ago. There is a known strategy for taking old and timeless products and "reincarnating" them and bringing them back to life, with great financial success. You may leave the product exactly as is, or you may want to change it slightly to "modernize" it. It is an option which definitely shouldn't be neglected.

Solve a small annoyance. Here is a unique concept. Do you have little pet peeves that just get you all flustered? Think about it for a minute. It could be anything trivial such as: loose shopping buggies at mall parking lots, doggy-do on your front lawn, bad breath, door-to-door salesmen, husband leaving the toilet seat up, toothpaste cap getting lost, telemarketers calling at dinner time, etc. etc. If you can solve one of these little issues creatively and cost efficiently, it could produce a big bank account in your name!

Upcoming event or interest cycle. When a very public event is about to take place, and the public has a growing interest in this event, it represents a valuable opportunity for lining your pockets with cash! Any major event causing the public to go into a frenzy may be the right arena for your creative product. Think of some of the major headlines in the past: Man walks on the moon, Mohammed Ali wins world heavy weight title, O.J. Simpson charged with murder, Michael Jackson arrested again, JFK assassinated, and so on. Can you think of a product that you can create and market quickly to meet a present or upcoming event of great interest?

One thing that you should realize when developing products around an event or interest cycle, is that you have to be prepared to work at mach speed! The event or cycle will come and go very quickly. Your product will be developed specifically to meet this market, and will have little value once the event has vanished from people's minds. I call this the **"hit-and-run marketing strategy"** —you get in quickly and get out with your cash in hand! It has tremendous earnings potential, but it is short-lived.

Sell a consumable item. In direct response, the biggest profits are made with repeat sales, not with selling one item. Therefore, one of your main goals of a direct marketer is to think of "add-on" products which you can create into a large product line. You might hit it big with only ONE high-priced revolutionary item – but the odds are greatly against you. For lasting success in this business, think of products that get used up and must be reordered. Or products that can be packaged in creative ways to create larger and more expensive items for future sales to your existing clientele. Some products that have reorder potential: vitamins and minerals, clothing lines, foods of any kind, cosmetics, hair products, skin care products. Thousands more can be added to this list.

ALL ABOUT CREATING A SERVICE BUSINESS

Serve them and they will come. More of American millionaires have created their wealth with service businesses than any other income vehicle. Face it. Consumers want to be served. They have unique needs and wants. Can you come up with a business that is a little bit different or better than the competition? Being creative with your business ideas has key advantages that can propel you to the front lines of an industry very quickly. Here are some areas and suggestions to assist you when creating your service business:

- Do it at a cheaper price.
- Offer better quality and service.
- Offer insurance if your competitors don't.
- Offer warranties and testimonials.
- Have longer warranties than your competitors.
- Give alternative payment options: check, cash, credit cards, internet banking, debit cards.
- Offer FREE parking. Valet parking.
- Offer longer hours and extra work days than the norm. Open on Sundays.
- 24 hour paging service. Use a cell phone. Be easily accessible.
- Free delivery, quicker delivery.
- Install a toll-free 1-800 number.
- Offer free inspections, free samples, free consultations.
- Give faster and more competent service.
- Customize your product line to fit all your different customers.
- Liberal return policies or strong money-back guarantees.
- Longer money-back guarantees.
- Increase your ordering methods: mail, phone, fax, internet, e-mail.
- Be more knowledgeable than the competition.
- Specialize in one core task and be the best at that.
- Offer payment plans or extended financing.
- Offer no-down-payment services.

Use the Yellow Pages to research competitors. Prior to starting any type of business that already has direct competitors, you should be prepared to do some careful research. The Yellow Pages is a gold mine of information just sitting there for you to sniff out information about your competitors. Look for the following:

- Any free offers that are used to generate leads (free estimates/consultations)
- Their contact information (surf through their web site)
- How long they have been in business
- How many store locations they have
- Store hours or operating hours (be more convenient than they are)
- Demographic area or locations that they service (look for areas they won't go to)
- Product and labor guaranties or warranties
- Discount specials that are offered (seniors discounts)
- The payment options that they offer (make sure to offer more options than they do)
- Any licenses, insurance or permits that are advertised

Send in the spies. One sneaky trick I like to use is to get one of my employees to call up my competition and pretend to be an interested shopper. My employee asks pertinent details such as: how they market their business, how they operate, what their prices are, how fast they can deliver, financing options, guarantees, and service options offered. Gathering this information allows us to come in to the market with a better offer, and in effect we also create our "Unique Selling Proposition."

Unique selling proposition. This is a key benefit which separates you from the crowd. It is what you do the best and your reputation or branding will be built around this key benefit. Have a look again at the above list for creating a unique business, send in your spies to gather as much information as you can on the competition, do any other necessary market research you will require, and then think of your unique selling proposition. For my builder agency business my proposition might be: "Unsurpassed personal service at rock-bottom prices." Or it could be "brilliant creative – quick turnaround." Do you get the message? You need to know what your positioning statement will be

*HOW TO CREATE AN UNLIMITED INCOME
SITTING AT HOME IN YOUR PAJAMAS*

so that you can build your advertising and marketing around this unique feature. A few more words... make sure your customers understand your statement, and make sure that it is simple. Also make sure that it is centered around your customer's needs and wants—not your own.

Type of service business to start. When choosing a service business, it makes sense to get into something with a huge future potential. Some of the hottest businesses to start are: desktop publishing or web site design, home health care, printing, marketing, advertising, consulting, promotions, public relations, financial planning, career counseling, educational services, computer services/software, import/export, communications, technology, e-commerce, and real estate. These are all high growth industries with huge future earnings potential. You don't want to be dead right off the bat by getting into an industry which is:

Matured: and loaded with competition battling it out with no profits in sight
Retiring: like shipping, oil, steel, railroads, mining
Obsolete: horse-drawn carriages, saddle-making, blacksmith business

Avoid the sole income-earner business. There are hundreds of businesses in income opportunity magazines like: gift basket services, carpet cleaning, duct cleaning, car detailing, and so on that are actually glorified "monkey-traps." You become the sole income-earner and run the business day and night. If you stop working the money stops coming in. This is exactly what you want to avoid. You don't want to buy yourself a job. Your goal is to create a business that can be run automatically with formulas, not with the owners' day-to-day labor. That's when you will create unlimited income, and also have the time to enjoy it!

The correct hourly rate. Do you want to make a truck-load of money in a service business? I'm not talking about a regular wage here, like $1,000 a week. I'm talking more like $3,000 a day. Well pay very close attention....this is extremely important. I struggled through many failed and mediocre businesses for over 10 years until I discovered this little secret...which all by itself has catapulted my income ten-fold. I wouldn't want you to waste that many years of your life to discover it on your own. So here goes:

BILL YOUR SERVICE OUT AT $100 AN HOUR OR MORE

This is a very powerful statement. Do not start a service business that you can't charge your customers at least $100/hour for. I would be even more comfortable at a rate closer to $150/hour. Charge more if your market will bear it. This is the secret for making the big bucks!

You probably know that many services like auto repair shops, electricians, plumbers and contractors are close to this rate already. But there are many other businesses still in the $30 - $50 dollar an hour range. And that is fine for them. They run out of retail establishments and have different overheads. You, as a direct marketer, will have your own unique expenses (which we will discuss shortly) that you will have to contend with. Can you make a profit billing out at $50 an hour? Sure you can. But it will be negligible. As mentioned above, I'm not interested in teaching you how to earn a measly pay, you can do that yourself by closing this book and getting a job. In fact, doctors, lawyers and other professionals get paid the executive hourly wages I'm advocating…so why shouldn't an entrepreneur such as yourself do the same?

A secondary issue of major importance, is to try to **hire employees to fulfill the services at a rate not higher than 1/4 of your hourly fee.** So if your fee is at $100/hour, you should be paying your employees no more than $25/hour—this is key. Following this advice, you will have enough mark-up to make a killing in direct marketing your service business. You will thank me for this later!

OTHER VERY IMPORTANT DIRECT MARKETING ISSUES

Beware of the seasonal product or service. When creating your future business, make sure it is not dependent on a certain season to bring in the bulk of the yearly income. For instance, seasonal businesses can be one of the following: snow removal, landscaping, decking, painting, Christmas ornaments, bathing suits, snowshoes, leisure crafts, motorcycles. And there are many more. Seasonal items and services do well for only a limited number of months out of the year (especially if you live in cold climates like Canada). They just are not steady income earners throughout the year. Own one of these babies and you will fully understand the term "feast or famine." The trick here is to avoid seasonal businesses altogether, or to start a number of "opposite seasonal businesses" so that when one dies down the other will be picking up steam.

Avoid fad items. Fad items are here today, gone tomorrow. You should avoid them like the plague. They are absolutely the most risky product to create and try to market. When creating your product or service make sure that it's focus is based around a need which is established, in great demand, and unchanging. One of these is nourishment (we all have to eat), another is shelter (we all need to live somewhere), another is toilets (we all need to expel). Fads are usually marketed to a tiny segment of the population, so if you create an idea that is geared to the masses, it has a good chance of living a long and productive life. How many "pet rocks" have you bought lately?

Know thy demographics. The fact is, you have to know who your customers are before you can market to them efficiently. You have to know their sex, their age, their income level, where they live, their ethnic background, their education level, their salary range, the color of their underwear! You have to gather as much information as humanly possible, so that you can tailor your marketing plan to fit your customers needs. Other very important questions that will require answering are:

- Where do my customers shop?
- Are they prime candidates for direct response advertising?
- What kind of newspapers and magazines do they read?
- How can I reach my potential customers?
- How can I reach them more affordably?
- What is the quickest way to reach them?

Furthermore, I suggest that you look through a copy of *American Demographics* or do a search on the internet for it. It is a large book which lists different demographic sections for both Canada and the United States. This popular book has now been turned into a magazine which features advanced marketing strategies, detailed diagrams and key data that will assist marketers in targeting their exact population segment. So do some initial research prior to throwing your whole body and soul into an idea, just to make sure that: **a viable market does exist, can be easily identified, and can be marketed to quickly and economically.**

THE GOLDEN RULE IN DIRECT MARKETING IS THAT YOUR PRODUCT MUST BE MARKED-UP AT LEAST 10 TIMES FOR EXCEPTIONAL PROFITS!

Without question, the above heading ranks at the top of the importance list if you wish to succeed in the Direct Marketing business. Read that heading to yourself a few times, so it sinks in. I'm sure you have seen advertisements of "wholesalers" or "distributors" where they sell you their products and to hundreds of other mail order operators as well. These wholesaling companies typically provide you with full color catalogues with their complete product lines, imprinted with your company name on the outside. They drop ship your orders for you (this means that when you receive an order, they mail the product directly from their warehouse to the customer). Your customer never realizes that a wholesale company is involved in the picture as a "hidden middle-man." The bulk of their products are figurines and other knick-knacks. Mark ups are generally two to three times the initial price of the product. For example: if you buy a ceramic doll from a wholesaler for $3.00, your retail price to your customers will be approximately $9.00. The reality of the situation is that you will never have enough of a built-in markup this way so that you can pay for your advertising and still make a decent profit. It just isn't possible. I strictly advise you to steer clear of these "wholesaling" business opportunities.

To understand the concept of markups, you have to fully comprehend the effects of your products "complete cost" and also the "cost per order" of your advertising.

Complete cost. Even if you create a product of your own invention and you manufacture it at a cost of $10.00, you still have to add in the other costs that are involved in getting your product to the customer. The complete costs of a product include:

1. **The manufacturing of your product (both labor and materials)**
2. **Shipping materials such as boxes, tape and bubble wrap (and the labor involved)**
3. **Shipping and handling, courier or postage costs**
4. **Returns, lost items, and bad debts**

Once you factor in all of the above amounts you will probably find out that the original price of your product that you had calculated at $10.00 is actually incorrect, and the complete cost is $15.00. You now have a clear picture of what your product actually costs you to manufacture, package and ship to your client.

HOW TO CREATE AN UNLIMITED INCOME SITTING AT HOME IN YOUR PAJAMAS

Cost per order. This is another very important calculation that you always have to keep accurate track of. If you spend $1,000 on advertising your product, which eventually you receive 100 inquiries from, and you finally make a sale to 10 of these prospects, your "cost per order" will be $100 ($1,000 divided by 10 = $100 CPO). Each one of those customers cost you $100 of cold hard cash to land them as a paying client! Wow, pretty expensive you say? You are absolutely right!

Now imagine if you were selling the above $15.00 product to one of these customers. Taking the ten times mark up factor, you would be retailing your product for $150.00. Since your cost per order is $100.00 and your product is $150.00, congratulations…you have a net profit left over of $50.00. Welcome to the Direct Marketing field! You should now begin to see the importance of having the correct combination of the:

1. **Lowest advertising cost per order**
2. **Highest markup possible (10 times)**
3. **Correct pricing of your product**

Having the above correct combinations in place will not assure you of 100% success in the Direct Marketing business, but it will surely put the odds in your favor. As this business involves a wide array of variables that have to be combined correctly to have any measurable success, you will need the correct markup in your products to be able to handle the mistakes you will inevitably make.

We have discussed "cost per order" and the "correct mark-up" for your products. It's time now to get into the details of:

PRICING YOUR PRODUCTS FOR SUCCESS

Have you decided on the price that you will charge for your product? I SURE HOPE NOT! One thing you must always remember in this business if you wish to succeed is that: **Your customers will set your prices for you!** The importance of this cannot be stressed enough. Who are you to know what your customers are willing to spend for your offer? I can tell you something with complete confidence—you will always be shocked to find out what your customers are willing to pay for a product that you bring into the marketplace. Many times it will be higher than what you assumed, and sometimes it will be lower. The only way to know for sure what the market will bear is by "testing" your offering, and this is something we will cover in the next chapter.

One thing I can tell you with extreme certainty, is that you should do your best to market only **products which you can retail for $100 or more**. Personally, I would not market anything less than $200. Gone are the days of advertising a widget for $2.00 in the hopes of getting millions of orders and becoming rich. With the sky-rocketing costs of direct marketing (and other factors) it is becoming increasingly difficult to make an outstanding profit with products priced under $100. In my experience, I would say that an ideal price range would be between $200 - $500…and more if you can get it!

Please consider the following factors which affect the pricing of direct response products today:

1. High costs of shipping and postage. These prices go up without a doubt, every single year and sometimes at astronomical percentages.

2. Advertiser competition. Your potential customers are blitzed on a daily basis by hundreds of offers for them to spend their money on. This lowers the response rate to your offerings, as you have to compete for the customer's attention. Do a direct mailing today, and expect to get a 1% response rate. If you mail 100 offers you will receive only one response! Needless to say, this is quite disappointing.

3. Growing costs of printing. All production costs involved in printing your offer, whether it is a full color brochure, or a number of letter sized pages, increases at an alarming rate each year. This too, makes it extremely difficult to show a profit in the direct response business.

Please don't get discouraged. I will be revealing to you advanced strategies for maximizing your response rates, as well as destroying the competition (in later chapters). In the present Direct Marketing economic conditions, it will be impossible to break even on a $40 product. Realistically, a minimal profit will be realized on a $60 product. With a $100 product you have a fighting chance of making a healthy profit. Get into the marketing of products in the $500 price range, and you have the makings of a very realistic $300,000-a-year income. That should get your heart beating faster!

One final tip: Use even–odd pricing strategies with lower priced items. This means if your product will be priced at $300 – lower it to $299.95 (subconsciously it sounds cheaper). If you are selling high priced items, keep them at an even price, so as not to "cheapen them" in the eyes of your prospect.

*HOW TO CREATE AN UNLIMITED INCOME
SITTING AT HOME IN YOUR PAJAMAS*

PLANT YOUR OWN MONEY-TREE: THE AMAZING WEALTH-BUILDING SECRETS OF INFORMATION PRODUCTS

I purposely left this category of product/service until the end of the chapter so I can give it the undivided attention it truly requires! The creating and marketing of information is probably the number one wealth-generating strategy to sell via direct response advertising. The advantages far outweigh other traditional products or services. Here is a partial list of the advantages: Ease of creation, effortless to research, affordable to test, has global marketing potential, very little overhead and start-up costs required (can be printed on demand), huge markup possibilities, highly valuable (you customers will pay a high price for it), home-based and extremely mobile, copyright and intellectual property protection, and lasting benefits—as information can be recorded, printed and stored for a lifetime!

ENDLESS POSSIBILITIES IN INFORMATION PRODUCTS

The fact is that people are hungry for information, and willing to pay top dollar for it. Any knowledge or skill which you possess, or can gain control of, has the power to be packaged into an information products empire. What categories do information products fall into? There is an endless list which can be combined and formatted to fit your own requirements, but here is a listing of the most common:

Audio tapes, CD's and DVD's, books, newsletters, magazines, E-letters and E-zines (via e-mail), reports, calendars, manuals, workbooks, booklets, games, video VHS tapes, seminars, telephone conference calls, hands-on training, posters, 900 numbers, consulting, home study courses, interactive internet systems.

The potential combinations of the above ideas is just limitless! Your goal as an information marketer, is to attract as many interested customers into your web (with enticing FREE offers) and then keep them there for the long term. Start off by offering free information or free products, and work up to higher valued back-end products/services in the years to come. The listings shown above can be broken down into six categories: **Telephone, Video, Digital, Live, Audio and Print.** They should start as a free item, move to a $10-$20 item, then to a $200 package, then up to a $500 home-study course, and finally up to a combination of hands-on material in the $1,000 + range. Let's have a look at each separate category to see how we can move from the lowest priced item to the highest priced items.

Telephone – start with a free call (1-800 number live or taped), move into 900 numbers (live or taped), and finally to one-on-one consulting or conference calls.

Video – start with a free video, sell a two video set, sell a five video kit, move into taped seminar videos business-in-a-kit.

Digital – start with a free CD/DVD, partial e-mail book, online books, books on CD/DVD, software, some kind of interactive grouping.

Live – free something (seminar, speech, consultation, appearance), move to a four–hour half-day seminar, evening seminar, one–day seminar, all inclusive weekend get-away seminar, one week vacation life-transforming seminar, one-on-one client consultation.

Audio – free cassette, two tape kit, 10 cassette package, 20 tape audio home-study course.

Print – start with a free (report, newsletter, brochure, direct mail piece), move into a book - booklet - calendar - poster or game, move up to 300–page detailed manual, some kind of home-study course.

CREATE CLEVER COMBINATIONS OF INFORMATION PRODUCTS

With the creative combination of the above items, you can sell exactly the same information but at different price categories, and different values (as believed by the client). Following are some ideas to get you thinking about the creative combining possibilities:

Newsletter, booklet, 1 video, 1 audio cassette = $75
10 Special reports, 3 audio cassettes, a video, and a book = $100
200 page manual, workbook, 5 audio cassettes, 3 videos, 900 number taped
    = $300

*HOW TO CREATE AN UNLIMITED INCOME
SITTING AT HOME IN YOUR PAJAMAS*

Detailed manual, 5 CD's, 5 videos, 10 audio cassettes, telephone consultation = $600
Weekend seminar, business-in-a-kit to take home = $1,500

Each package can be tailored to fit the different clients you will be attracting to your business. Some clients will be passive low-end purchasers, others will be meat-and-potatoes types seeking detailed information, and a few will be top professionals and presidents of large companies seeking the highest-value and hands-on training you have available. Each category of audience will have different needs and varied price budgets which you should be able to satisfy by cleverly combining your information. **So keep in mind that the knowledge which you possess (or can research, borrow, or create) has incredible value...and somebody else who does not have this same expertise will pay you handsomely to attain it in a fast and affordable fashion!** You can take this guarantee straight to the bank.

KEEP YOUR SERVICE AND PRODUCT IDEAS CONFIDENTIAL

In the excitement of the creation or development phase, many beginner direct marketers rush out to reveal their ideas to friends and relatives. Their beliefs are that they will receive some kind of great or worldly advice about how to sell their ideas to the waiting marketplace. There is no better way to destroy your motivation and plans than unveiling your ideas to people who are not experienced direct marketing gurus! Let's face it, friends and relatives might have good intentions, but they lack the evaluating skills and advice of an expert in this field. And trust me, direct marketing is a very intricate field with a complex weave of variables which must be perfected in order to achieve a notable success. So I advise you to:

A. keep your ideas to yourself
B. move forward with the creation of your plans
C. acknowledge that your near-misses will give you the experience to make the right decisions in the future.

Chapter 3
Creating Compelling Offers and Testing Your Ideas

In this chapter we will be learning all about testing our ideas, writing attention-grabbing ads and offers, and creating strategic Direct Marketing campaigns. This information will allow you to gain confidence in the viability of your idea, and to create winning advertising promotions that will fill your mailbox full of cash!

DRY MARKET TESTING

"Dry Market Testing" is probably the most unique benefit of the direct response business! Testing your idea for free, or with small classified ads will save you years of disappointment, wasted time, and thousands of squandered dollars. So this is what Dry Market Testing is: You test your idea, product or service before you jump head first into the creation stages. You test before you even build your first prototype. You test even before you register your business name. Testing comes second, after the little "idea" light bulb goes off in your brain. Dry testing is perfectly legal, but I would recommend that you contact the Federal Trade Commission to double check in your state or province.

Thousands of inventors fall prey to this mistake of not testing prior to developing their ideas. As mentioned earlier in my book, most patents never make it into the market place. Therefore, I urge you to test prior to creating your own dud, the time and money you will save can be used for other worthwhile ideas in the future.

Testing is performed by sending out "Silent Salesmen" to test the market and discover whether there is a **DEMAND** for your idea. Their initial goal is to achieve the highest response possible from an offer, ultimately proving that your idea will be **PROFITABLE**. Silent salesmen can be:

1. Small classified ads in newspapers
2. Direct mail pieces
3. E-mail and internet marketing
4. Fax broadcasting
5. Delivery of printed material door-to-door
6. Telemarketing and voicemail can also be used in conjunction with the proceeding, to reinforce the selling atmosphere.

Note: each of the above marketing categories can be used alone or combined with each other to create unique strategic campaigns. Prior to getting into each of the above in detail, I wish to discuss some other important aspects of Direct Marketing which will give you a solid base of understanding.

THE MOST POWERFUL, ATTENTION-GRABBING WORDS IN MARKETING

Because we will be learning how to create our own advertisements, direct mail pieces and other marketing material as we go along, it is extremely important to be aware that certain words generate actions from potential prospects. These words entice the prospect to take notice and then force him/her to take action. Study the following list of powerful words. Use them in your ads, headlines, classified ads, print materials, telemarketing scripts, and all other direct marketing promotions. These words will give you the competitive "sizzle" needed to succeed in this business.

A

Absolutely, Advice, Amazing, Announcing, A Sampler of…, Affordable, A Gallery of…, Alert, Allure, Acquisition-Minded, Appreciate, Appeal, Astonishing, At Last…, Attractive, Attention, Authentic, Avoiding

B
Bargain, Be, Beautiful, Believe, Benefit, Best, Better, Big Blowout, Boom, Brand-name, Breakthrough, Billboard, Block-busting, Brain-picking, Bright, Budget Buy, Buy Direct, Bottom Line, Bonanza, Brave

C
Call, Care, Challenge, Choose, Cost Clearance, Closeout, Compare, Compelling, Competitive, Complete, Comprehensive, Compromise, Concept, Confidential, Convenient, Crucial

D
Daring, Delicious, Delivered, Dependable, Deserve, Destiny, Development, Direct, Discount, Discover, Distinguished, Dividends, Drastically, Dynamic

E
Easy, Edge, Effective, Endorsed, Endurance, Energy, Enterprising, Envision, Event, Excellent, Exciting, Exclusive, Exercising, Expert, Exploit, Extra, Extravaganza

F
Fabulous Fact, Family, Famous, Fantastic, Fascinating, Fast, Feel, Flex, Flourish, Focus, Foothold, Forecast, Fortune, Formula, Free, Freedom, Fresh, Full, Financial Freedom, Fueling, Fundamentals

G
Gain, Gaining On, Genuine, Get, Gift, Gigantic, Give, Go, Great, Growth, Guarantee, Gut Feelings

H
Have, Health, Hello, Help, Helpful, Here's, Heritage, Highest, Honest, Hot Property, How-to, Huge, Hurry, High Tech, Hybrid

I
Incredible, Imagination, Important, Improve, Independence, Inflation-busting, Informative, Innovative, Insatiable, Interesting, Introduce, Investigative, Investment, Inviting

J
Just in Time

K
Knowledge, Keep

L
Last Minute, Largest, Late-breaking, Latest, Launching, Learn, Liberated, Lifeblood, Lifetime, Limited, Lively, Longevity, Look, Low, Love, Loving, Luxury

M
Make Money, Magic, Mainstream, Mania, Masterpiece, Measure Up, Merit, Miracle, Modern, Monitor, Monumental, More, Most

N
Need, New, News, Nest Egg, Next Frontier, No-risk, Nostalgic, Novel, Now

O
Obsession, Offer, Official Only, Open, Opportunity, Outstanding, Overrated

P
Personalized, Perspective, Philosophy, Pioneering, Please, Popular, Portfolio, Positive, Powerful, Practical, Preppie, Price, Present, Prevent, Professional, Profit, Profitable, Promise, Protect, Proof, Proud, Proven

Q
Qualified, Quality, Quick

R
Rare, Ready, Real, Reassurance, Receive, Recommend, Recruit, Redeem, Reduce, Refer, Refund, Relax, Reliable, Relief, Remarkable, Reminiscent, Responsible, Reputation, Results, Reward, Reveal, Revisited, Revolutionary, Rich, Right, Romance, Rush

S
Safety, Satisfaction, Save, Savvy, Secret, Secure, Security Selected, Selection, Self-confidence, Sensational Service, Sex, Show Me, Shrewd, Simple, Skill, Slash, Smart, Smile, Soar, Special, Specialize, Spiral, Spotlight, Start, Starter-kit, Startling, Step-by-step, Success, Super, Sure-fire, Survival

T
Take, Tax-resistant, Team, Tech Revolution, Technology, Terrific, Tested, Test Drive, Thank You, Time, Timely, Today, Top Dog, Traces, Tremendous, Trust, Try

U
Ultimate, Unbelievable, Unconditional, Understand, Unique, Under-priced, Unlimited, Unlock, Unreal, Up Scale, Useful

V
Valuable, Value, Vast, Vital

W
Want, Warranty, Wealth, Welcome, Willpower, Win, Wise, Wonderful, Word-of-mouth, Worth

Y
Yes, You, Youthful

Z
Zingers

ALL ABOUT OFFERS

Your offer is one of the most critical strategies in your marketing arsenal. Your offer must be crystal clear, simple, risk-free and of great value to your prospect. What is an offer? It can be described as:

You will receive "such and such"....all you have to do is "this and this." It is the heart of your selling strategy. It describes what the prospect will receive from you, and what he/she has to do in order to attain it. Your offer should contain: information about the product/service, the price, any discounts or free items, the length and type of guarantee, believable testimonials, ordering alternatives, and various payment options.

There are two basic formats for offers that are available for you to use:

The Soft Offer. This is the most commonly used offer, many times referred as a "Two-Step" or "Lead Generation" offer. In this instance, the prospect is asked to respond to some kind of additional information or free package. There is no risk of having to speak to a sales representative or having one call in the future. In this instance, the prospect jumps up from the crowd and identifies himself as a very interested lead. He has a need for your product/service, but does not want to be pestered by a salesperson, he wants to receive more detailed info on your company and then take his time to buy…on his own terms.

In direct mail campaigns, this Two-Step method is probably the best one to use. It allows you to send more information (which is actually your well-written sales letter), to describe your product more fully and make a sale. In most of my marketing campaigns, I have employed this two-step method with great success.

Usually a two-step direct mail offer will be composed of:
1. **An outside envelope (probably a #10)**
2. **A sales letter, personally signed**
3. **A brochure/catalogue detailing the features of your product/service**
4. **A separate order form**
5. **A return envelope (probably a #8)**

The soft offer works well when: you do not have employees or in-house sales reps, you have a superb selling package already established, your product is so technical or too difficult to be described in a small ad, and selling immediately is out of the norm of your particular category of product/service.

The Hard Offer. In this offer, the prospect is asked to make a sale immediately, send cash up-front, or be subject to speaking to a sales agent either in person or over the telephone. The hard offer is one way of weeding out the "tire kickers" or the prospects who may not be ready to be sold to immediately. The hard or "One-Step" offer, requests the prospect to take a solid step in buying your product/service right now, not down the road.

This type of offer does not work well with products that require detailed information, explanation, or a new product on the market which the prospect will need to be educated fully on. Hard offers were used many years ago when selling small, simple widgets, $2 or $4 items (usually anything priced under $15).

When putting together a hard offer, be aware that you will have to list or achieve the following items in your ad:

1. **A powerful headline**
2. **Ad copy that creates interest in the reader**
3. **Copy must describe both benefits and features of your product**
4. **A strong desire must be reinforced**
5. **Strong testimonials from past buyers**
6. **The longest money-back guarantee you can offer**
7. **The price**
8. **Do the selling and make the sale**
9. **Use some sort of keyed code to track your ads**

You will notice how difficult it is to create a small, inexpensive ad listing all of the above items. And as stated earlier, I would not recommend selling a product priced below $100, so a hard offer will probably not be suitable for your needs.

The hard offer works well when you have excellent sales reps on hand to close the sale, your product is simple and easily sold in a quick conversation or in one ad, your market does not want printed material, or there is some free inspection or trial offer involved in the sales process.

COMBINING BOTH HARD AND SOFT OFFERS

One neat trick that you should try to use is to include both a hard and soft offering at the same time. You stress one important offer throughout your ad or sales literature, but end with the other offer as an alternative. This way you target both prospects: The ones who are "hot" right now, and those who are "fence sitters."

*HOW TO CREATE AN UNLIMITED INCOME
SITTING AT HOME IN YOUR PAJAMAS*

THE POWER OF "THE FREE BAIT OFFER"

The undisputed truth is that people love to get things for free. I think it is a huge mistake if you do not include something for FREE in all of your offers. It can be a free consultation, free gift, free booklet, free trial offer, free information kit, free recorded message, etc. Believe it or not, adding something of value which is FREE can boost your response by over 200 to 400%!

I remember when I was marketing an informational home-study course, I received quite a good response rate from my lead-generating ads. I decided to test the strength of my campaign by adding a "free, exciting one-hour cassette" and the increase in responses was approximately 400%. Yes folks, that is four times the previous number of inquiries I had received! Audio cassettes, videos, and now CD's all make excellent free gift offers. These recording formats are also very cheap to duplicate, so costs should never be an issue for you. It's funny, many people do not like to read, but will listen to or watch a one-hour sales presentation if given the opportunity.

One important detail which bears mentioning here is that you should strive to always include a "dollar value" along with your free bait offer to further solidify to your prospects that this is truly a once in a lifetime opportunity. If for example, you are giving away three free videos, you might want write a sentence like this in your sales literature: take advantage of our offer and order within the next two weeks to receive these three exciting videos – AN $80 VALUE…yours absolutely FREE!"

THE FREE RECORDED MESSAGE

This is probably the most amazing strategy available to direct marketers today. The strategy of listing in your ads that the prospect can call in to listen to a "free recorded message." It is very disarming, as prospects are bombarded with hard-sell sales pitches on a daily basis. The fact is, that a prospect may be extremely interested in your offer, but he may be terrified of having to face a sales rep on the other end of the telephone. The free recorded message allows him to call at his "comfort level" with "no-risk" of sales pressure what-so-ever. You are also making it very easy for him to respond. It is much easier to pick up the phone and listen to a free recorded message, rather than put a reply form in an envelope, place a stamp on it and take it to a post office box.

What the prospect is asked to do is call and listen to a brief, friendly greeting and description of your product/service. The prospect is then asked to leave his name, address, and perhaps his e-mail address, to receive further FREE information on your product. You may even wish to add some kind of FREE gift that the prospect can keep just for leaving his contact information.

Notice what just took place by the prospect:

He/she has read your ad completely
Made the decision to phone
Stayed on line long enough to listen to the message
Recorded his/her contact information

You can bet that this is a very interested candidate for your sales information! After leaving his contact info, make sure to respond immediately by sending your sales package.

USING A TOLL-FREE 1-800 NUMBER BOOSTS RESPONSES

The use of a 1-800 number will tremendously boost the responses you receive in all of your offerings. You should have a toll-free line set up immediately. Whether it is a one-step offer where prospects are asked to call and speak to a representative, or using the "free recorded message" strategy, the 1-800 number will increase responses dramatically. Make sure to indicate in your ad or sales material that it is a "Toll-free" or "Free Call."

Furthermore, if you can arrange it with your phone service provider, try to get a toll-free number that relates to your business and is easily remembered by your prospects. For example, if you run a business geared around gourmet treats for dogs, your 1-800 number might be: 1-800-DOG-MEAL.

VOICE MAIL: YOUR FULL–TIME SECRETARY

The amazing thing about the "free recorded message" and the availability of voice mail systems, is that you can actually create a 7-day-a-week, 24-hour a day, secretary! This strategy is ideal for people wishing to test their business idea while they are still employed at their regular day job. This strategy is truly an **Automation Perfected Strategy**.

HOW TO CREATE AN UNLIMITED INCOME SITTING AT HOME IN YOUR PAJAMAS

Picture this scenario:

You place a classified ad which ends in a "free recorded message." Your prospects call in at their own leisure, at all ours of the day and night. You can be working at your full-time day job and your voice mail will be recording your leads. You check your messages during your lunch break, and/or after work, and write down the contact info. After work, you stuff your envelopes and mail them out, or send your free information package (sales offer) via fax or e-mail.

With the advanced technology today, it is possible to have multiple voice mail lines so your respondents will never have to hear a busy signal. Eight hundred numbers, as well as other advanced storage and retrieval methods, can be added very easily to the voice mail services. Look for a suitable voice mail supplier in your Yellow Pages, or do a search on the internet. At a minimum, call your telephone company and have voicemail added to your phone service.

ALL ABOUT GUARANTEES

Nothing will strengthen your direct marketing offers more powerfully, than a solid and long money-back guarantee. Think for a moment how a potential mail order customer feels prior to placing an order with your company. The prospect has never heard of you before, has not seen you, never spoken to you, and is taking your word that you will send him his product after he parts with his cash. There may be a bit of anxiety involved on his part. Giving the prospect a guarantee reassures him.

A 30-day money-back guarantee is typical in mail order. If you can shoot for 60 or 90 days, this is even better. Some mail order courses advise to give one-year guarantees, but you have to be careful with very long time spans as prospects may abuse the lengthy periods. A two-week guarantee is not enough time for the prospect to decide if the product is worthwhile. Whatever way you look at it, a longer guarantee will produce better results than a short guarantee (or no guarantee at all). One final tip: make your guarantees totally unconditional...or "no strings attached."

MAKE YOUR OFFERS LIMITED

Putting a time limit on your offers will force prospects to make a quick response, so as they don't miss the available opportunity. If you do not put a deadline on your offers, prospects will just put your offer aside thinking they will respond later. More than likely they never will. If you don't get them while they're "hot" and interested in your offering, chances are you will never make the sale.

You will have to calculate the mailing time of your material (if it is sent via mail), so as to give the prospect enough time to receive your offering and read it over. Keeping the time limit short (like two weeks) will add urgency to the offer. You might even want to go up to 20 days as the high end of your time limits. Make sure your offers sound credible and honest.

Following is a number of examples of limited offers you may wish to use:

- Get a free gift if you order within the next 2 weeks
- This introductory price will be raised in 2 weeks
- This offer is valid for the next 20 days
- Only 1,000 products available, order by so & so date
- Fall special 10% discount, order within the next 3 weeks

START DEVISING YOUR OWN CREATIVE OFFER

When creating your own offer, try to concentrate on these three items:
1. **The product/service**
2. **The payment terms**
3. **Any free premiums/gifts**

Do your best to make it as risk-free as possible to the prospect, as this will increase the response to your offering. Let's investigate some well-known offers which you may want to use:

- You need not send money now, we will bill you later
- Make 3 easy payments of 39.99, billed monthly to your credit card
- Order now and send a post-dated check, we will cash it in 30 days
- Send us payment up front, and receive the product
- No-money-down terms available, we will finance you
- Try a small sample for free, we will send you the larger item later
- Pay $10 for the trial offer, and we will deduct this from your next order

*HOW TO CREATE AN UNLIMITED INCOME
SITTING AT HOME IN YOUR PAJAMAS*

- Order our product, and receive a free valuable gift
- Pay cash up front, our product is money-back guaranteed

THE BEST MONTHS TO ADVERTISE

Before you run out and start spending your hard-earned money on ads to test your offer, you have to be aware of the best direct marketing months to advertise. Certain months have been proven to be big winners for mail order, while others can be financially devastating. The summer months are the worst, as people are away on vacation and do not respond well to direct response offerings. Never advertise before a long weekend (Thanksgiving, Easter, etc.). Right before and during Christmas holidays is also a complete write-off.

You will find below a listing of the best months to advertise in, and the ones to avoid.

Best months: January, February, March, April, September, October, November
Months to avoid: May, June, July, August, December

PEOPLE BUY BECAUSE OF BENEFITS – NOT FEATURES

Tailor all your advertising materials around one simple, and clearly defined benefit that the prospect will receive when he orders your product or service. Features are required, as they give the full details of what will be purchased. Features are explained in your brochure, or in the body copy of your sales letter. However, people frequently make a purchase decision that is based entirely upon emotions and benefits.

For example, If I was to write a headline promoting a new subdivision for seniors, I would use a headline such as this:

Live the lifestyle you've always dreamed of, at a time when you can enjoy it!

This is a big benefit. I'm promoting the "lifestyle" amenities available near the home site, and I will reinforce this theme with a handful of photos showing seniors enjoying all aspects of lifestyle activities. I would not mention gas fireplaces, ceramic tiles, 9–foot ceilings, or brass light fixtures, as these are features of the home which will be discussed at the sales office. But to get the prospects to the sales office… we advertise the biggest benefit: The lifestyle choice! Did I make my point?

HIDDEN PROFITS IN NICHE MARKETS

A niche is a small fragment of the population which is not being serviced properly, is abused, or just plainly forgotten. Here is a blessing in disguise, for you to dominate this niche market and make a killing. The reality is, you cannot reach a mass market properly. The budget to do it thoroughly, is definitely out of your reach. In other words: you have just created a mass appeal item, can you afford a full-page ad in the National Enquirer, or a full-blown infomercial to market your item? I think not. But you can surely afford a few classified ads in a niche publication or newspaper, right? Yes, I think so. A dedication on your part to focus on niche markets, will prove to be very advantageous. Think small. Smallness has its advantages.

ALL ABOUT LISTS

This is an area that will make or break your advertising campaign. You can have the most wonderful offer in the world, but if you send it to the wrong list of prospects your campaign will be a total failure. Your main goal as a beginner direct marketer is to locate prospects who you can transform into sales. Generating leads, compiling them on your own, or renting them from a list broker, are all methods of attaining possible prospects. I will now provide you with the most common lists available, ranked from best to worst.

- **House List.** This is the most valuable and potent list. It is the one which you probably do not have right now. The house list is a listing of people who have purchased from you in the past, or have shown an interest to your offerings in the past. You can place classified ads in newspapers to generate "leads." The prospects that call and are interested, are recorded as part of your "leads" house list. Keep your "leads" house list separate from actual "purchasers" of your house list.
- **Compiled List.** This is a list that you create yourself by doing a search on

the internet. If you have a product idea already, and know who your target market is, you can probably do a search for ASSOCIATIONS or DIRECTORIES of your specialized market. These listings will show names, addresses, and other contact info. Use this information to compile your own list. I have compiled my own lists for years, and find it to be a very effective way of building a good quality list.

- **Response Lists.** A response list is one where purchasers have bought products similar to your own by being attracted by similar marketing methods. Response lists are of better than normal quality, and so, cost a little more than regular lists. Try to find out as much as you can about the response list. Things like: how often purchasers bought in the past, the dollar amount spent, and when they last bought.
- **Other Lists.** These can include: credit card lists, attendee lists, database lists, membership lists, fund raising lists, subscription lists, sweepstakes lists. I would not recommend any of these, as the quality (many times) is surprisingly poor. You are treading on thin ice here…so be cautious!

THE IMPORTANCE OF HEADLINES

I can't think of a more critical item in your direct marketing campaign, than a powerful and attention-grabbing headline. Whether you are writing a classified ad, a brochure, a sales letter, or a fax promo, you will need to craft a bold headline capable of stopping the reader in his tracks and pulling him into the remaining copy material.

Spend at least 80% of your time in creating your headlines and 20% in writing the following sub-heading and body copy. After you are finished writing your headline, leave it alone for a day or so and come back to review it later. The break will offer you clear and fresh thinking ideas to revamp the headline.

Make sure to make a colossal promise, or guarantee a huge benefit in your headline. Adding in a touch of one of the basic human desires will also strengthen the headline. Use as many of the attention-grabbing words (listed earlier) in your headline, like: FREE, AMAZING, INCREDIBLE, RICHES, YOU, etc.

Your headline must have "Stopping Power" and "Pulling Power" to guide readers to read the rest of the copy. You have to catch the readers attention, make your promise or benefit, and force the reader to keep reading! Here are some tips to assist you in writing great headlines:

- Ask a question in your headline.
- Use the magical word: "FREE" in your headline
- Use the words: "YOU" or "YOUR" to personalize your headline
- Use as many of the "attention-grabbing" words as you can
- Use a bold and important subhead under your headline
- Use SEX in your headline (if it is relevant to your product/service)
- Make a boast or a dare in your headline
- Start with a HOW-TO headline
- Make a big promise or highlight the biggest benefit of your product/service
- Use a celebrity name or testimonial in your headline
- Reveal a secret in your headline
- Create curiosity from your prospects
- Surprise the prospect and catch them off guard
- Craft your headline so it reads just like a news headline (short and to the point)
- Use larger or bolder type to highlight important points in the headline
- Create a "story" or "dream" in your headline
- Be honest and sincere in your headline
- Use exclamation points and underlines in your headline

Looking at the above advice, you should begin to understand how you can go about creating your own powerful and clever headlines. Consequently, I will now list some well-known and very successful headlines to get your creative juices flowing further:

The Lazy Man's Way To Riches
How I Improved My Memory In One Evening
How To Win Friends And Influence People
Often A Bridesmaid, Never A Bride
Is The Life Of A Child Worth $1 To You?
Guaranteed To Go Through Ice, Mud Or Snow -- Or We Pay The Tow!
How A "Fool Stunt" Made Me A Star Salesman
They Laughed When I Sat Down At The Piano...
But Then I Started To Play!

HOW TO CREATE AN UNLIMITED INCOME
SITTING AT HOME IN YOUR PAJAMAS

If You Read Nothing Else – Read This
Do You Sincerely Want To Be Rich?
The Secret To Being Wealthy
Have You Ever Seen A Grown Man Cry?
How To Burn Off Body Fat, Hour-By-Hour!
Stop Dreaming And Start Making Money
Imagine Me – Holding An Audience Spellbound For 30 Minutes
Is Your Home Picture-Poor?

THE A.I.D.A. PRINCIPLE

This standard Direct Marketing principle should be used in writing both your headlines and all copy in your advertisements. These are the four core and integral goals which you should be striving for when creating your advertising material.

- A – ATTENTION: You have grab the prospects attention and stop him dead in his tracks
- I – INTEREST: Your wording must create an interest in the prospect to read on
- D – DESIRE: Listing all the benefits and features should create a desire in the prospect
- A – ACTION: You have to end with some kind of action or sale taking place

PIECING IT ALL TOGETHER – THE SILENT SALESMEN

You have just learnt the main aspects of putting together a successful "Silent Salesman" marketing campaign. Attention-grabbing words, offers, the free recorded message, voice mail, guarantees, limited offers, best months to advertise, benefits versus features, niche markets, lists, headlines and the AIDA principle…all combined together will give you a solid foundation so you can start devising your "Silent Salesman." Let's discuss the "Silent Salesmen" in detail.

SMALL CLASSIFIED ADS IN NEWSPAPERS

This category of small classified ads (or "word" ads) is one that I just love to death, and continue to use on a daily basis with incredible success. In all likelihood, you too will probably reap the same benefits if you decide to use classified ads to advertise your new idea. Interestingly, there are over 7,000 newspapers across the United States alone, and newspaper listings can be found quickly by doing a search on the internet. An overview of the benefits, tips and advantages of classified advertising will now be revealed:

- **Immediate results.** If you place a classified ad today, you will know tomorrow if there is a demand for your offer. Unlike magazines that have a lead time of 1 – 1.5 months of having to wait for the magazine to be printed, newspapers are printed on a daily basis and you can place an ad the day before it will be published. You will receive instant results the day the newspaper comes out, and you can track your results and have a quick idea if your offer will be successful or not.
- **Extremely affordable.** One of the enticing features of this method of advertising is the low cost. Many newspapers charge around $20 - $40/day for a two-line ad, making it ideal for the budget of a beginning home-business entrepreneur. Always do your best to come within the newspapers "minimum" requirements, so as to keep your advertising risk as small as possible. A minimum "word" requirement (15 words?) or a minimum "line" requirement, will probably vary from paper to paper.
- **Start your headline with an "A."** Because classified ads are usually listed alphabetically, it will be a good idea to start with an "A" by itself or a word beginning with the letter "A." I like using the words: Astonishing, Amazing, or Absolutely. Go back and review the attention-grabbing words in this chapter when you are ready to draft your classified ad headline. Being at the top of the list, will assist your ad in being read (and possibly called on) first, before your competition gets called. Here are some sample classified ads so you can see how to word them to get top placement:

Absolutely fantastic new acne miracle cream. Remarkable results. Free recorded details and free test sample. Call now 1-800-BYE-ACNE.

*HOW TO CREATE AN UNLIMITED INCOME
SITTING AT HOME IN YOUR PAJAMAS*

Amazing master painters at bargain prices. Astonishing results guaranteed. Fast and free estimates. Licensed and insured. Call now 1-800-WE-PAINT.

- **Weeklies compared with dailies.** I have placed hundreds (if not thousands) of classified ads throughout my business career, and the results that I have compiled reveal that advertising in weekly, bi-weekly or throw-away newspapers always out-pull advertising in daily newspapers. I believe the reason for this phenomenon, is that the daily newspapers are usually a larger and more crowded medium, and your ad simply gets lost in the masses of competitors ads. I would only use daily newspapers to advertise for employment positions available within your company. Free community newspapers, or once-a-week to 3-times- a-week newspapers work best for promoting your product or service.
- **Bold or highlight the first few words of your headline.** Go for this additional cost if allowed by the newspaper, it will make your ad stand out from the crowd. Many newspapers will add this "bolding" feature for free. You may want to add a "gray shading" behind your headline too. Sometimes other creative additions can also be made, like special icons, graphics, or borders.
- **Frequency and repetition.** Many newspaper sales representatives will try to pressure you into a long-term commitment by waving the "discount carrot" in front of you, telling you it is cheaper if you prepay for a longer ad run (like running an ad weekly for 3 months). DON'T FALL FOR THIS TRAP! The whole idea with classified ads is to keep them cheap and test them fast, with no commitment on your part if you have a dud of an idea. Take it from me, running an ad continuously DOES NOT IMPROVE RESULTS…in fact, you will notice that your results will start tapering off the longer you run your ad. Run your ad once a week or twice a week to test the waters. Place your ad to run over the weekend rather than the middle of the week. Ask the sales rep which day of the week has the largest circulation, and advertise on that day. Make sure to avoid advertising during long-weekends.
- **Change your ad or take a break.** If you have a winning ad, try to run with it for as long as you can while still remaining profitable. If you notice a steep decline in the calls coming in, this is an indication that you should re-write your ad with a new headline and body copy. Taking a break and not advertising for a few weeks, and then coming back with a fresh new ad will add spark and generate new responses. Save your old successful ads and rotate them every once in while.

- **Keep it close to home.** Advertise only in newspapers which are nearest to your business location. Prospects closer to your location will be have a deeper trust level and will be easier to convert into paying customers. We will discuss expansion possibilities later on, but for now stay localized with your classified advertising.
- **Advertise in the proper heading.** One of the disadvantages of classified advertising is that depending on what your are trying to sell, prospects may not be actively searching the newspaper classifieds for that type of product or service. Especially if you are targeting a specific niche market, you will have a difficult time trying to narrow down the correct heading to place your ad in. It is common sense, that if you are targeting a mass audience you will do well advertising in the classifieds. However, do your best to place your ad under a heading that best describes or suits your product/service. This way, the readers that are searching for your business will be able to find you easily.
- **Choose the right niche publication.** If your idea is a specialized one targeted to a niche market, make sure to find publications that are relevant to this market. If you have a financial investment kit for seniors for example, you should seek out weekly seniors magazines to place your classified ads in. You shouldn't have a problem locating at least one senior's magazine in every major city.
- **Discover and reuse the "golden" publications.** The "golden" publications are newspapers that out-pull all other newspapers (sometimes combined) for some mysterious reasons. We don't care what those reasons are, but when you discover such a publication…keep running your ad there! Case in point: One of my "golden" local community papers generates 30 calls a week, while other papers pull in only five calls/week each. Consequently, a successful publication is an open playing field for you to advertise other business ideas in a well.
- **Quality of prospect will vary.** As you begin to place classifieds and receive phone calls, you will notice certain patterns forming. One of these noticeable patterns is that certain communities from your local area will generate better quality prospects. It may be a community in the West end, or perhaps the North end. And because a certain newspaper handles that specific area, you will notice that all respondents calling from that paper will be of higher caliber. The prospects may have a better education, higher income, and live in a more prestigious neighbourhood. Hence, they will be better qualified to purchase your product or service.

*HOW TO CREATE AN UNLIMITED INCOME
SITTING AT HOME IN YOUR PAJAMAS*

- **Ethnic Newspapers.** Don't overlook community ethnic papers as a viable additional marketing area. Each city will probably have it's own set of Hispanic, German, Greek, Italian, etc. community newspapers where you will be able to place your classified ad. The sales representative handling you account will even translate your ad into the preferred language. I have had excellent results advertising in these types of papers, and there is no question in my mind that you will too!
- **Test, track and call to action.** Classified ads are easy to test, so therefore, test on a continual basis. Test your offer, your headline, your copy, and any free promotions that you may be offering at that time. Set up a tracking system so you know which ads are the most effective (more on this in the next chapter). And finally, make sure to have a "call to action" and tell the prospect exactly what you would like him/her to do: call now, call for free recorded details, call for free information kit, etc.

DIRECT MAIL PIECES

Direct mail is one of the most effective ways to reach your target market with accurate focus. Its results can be easily tracked, measured and tweaked to make future mailings even more profitable. I strongly urge you to include direct mail as your flagship marketing medium when reaching out to your potential prospects. If you are looking for the perfect medium to create an "Automatic Business" then look no further. After compiling your own list of contacts or generating leads with small classified ads and the free recorded message, you can mail out your "silent salesman" direct mail package. There is no person-to-person sales contact required. Your expertly crafted package will do the selling for you, and your prospect will mail you their payment.

As a rule of thumb, direct mail has a proven arrangement of materials which must be put together in order to be successful. This grouping includes the following:

1. **An outside envelope**
2. **A sales letter**
3. **A brochure**
4. **A reply form and return envelope**

I will give you some brief but critical tips on each of these items to assist you in creating an effective package. By any means, these are not complete how-to guidelines, just excellent pointers to give you a good head start.

An outside envelope. The goal of the outside envelope is to look as personalized as possible. As you may have compiled your own list of contacts or perhaps purchased a list, you will be sending your package out unsolicited. Your biggest goal will be getting your package past the "gate-keeper" (secretary) and into the hands of the decision-maker. If your package is going unsolicited to a person rather than a company, your goal will still be to get the package opened rather than just tossed into the trash can. The following tips will help you accomplish this:

- Use a #10 standard white business envelope
- Make it look as personable as possible
- Hand-write the address of the prospect, rather than using labels (Your initial mailings will probably be under 1,000 so this will not be too cumbersome).
- Do not imprint any teaser copy on the outside envelope
- Do not use a clear window with writing underneath
- Do your best to include the prospect's name
- Use a regular first-class stamp, not a stamp machine

A sales letter. Perhaps the most critical item in your direct mail package will be the sales letter. This is the piece which will act as your master salesman. Use the following tips when creating your sales letter:

- One color letters are fine, making them photocopy friendly.
- Contrary to popular belief, long sales letters (without being boring) will outperform short sales letters. Make yours as long as required to explain the benefits of your idea to the prospect. Tell the prospect how and why your idea will solve his existing problem. Tell him how easily and quickly he/she will experience the desired benefits. Your sales letter can be from one page to approximately 30 pages in length. Many times I have had great success with sales letters in the area of 10 pages.
- Make your sales letter as personable as possible by using a typewriter rather than a laser printer. DO NOT handwrite your sales letter.
- Start with a powerful headline. You do not need an introduction like: dear reader, or dear friend.
- Do not use a company logo at the top of your first page; instead, include

HOW TO CREATE AN UNLIMITED INCOME
SITTING AT HOME IN YOUR PAJAMAS

your logo at the end of the sales letter. You want your headline to have its own individual space so as to do its job of grabbing the prospects attention.

• Include a strong sub-heading under your headline.

• After the sub-head jump right into your sales pitch, do not waste any time.

• Use short paragraphs of 15 words or less to make it easy for the prospect to keep reading. Use bold lettering, underlines, dashes, dots, hyphens to make your letter more interesting. Do not over do it with these symbols, as your prospect will feel as though they are being "yelled at." Use sub-heads throughout your sales letter so that the "skimmers" will absorb the main theme while reading quickly.

• Make your sales letter irresistible by adding in "juicy" free bonuses and gifts to entice the prospect to order now.

• Write in a simple format. Use a lot of "I" and "You" and "Your" through out your letter. Use the word "FREE" and as many of the other "Attention-grabbing" words as you can muster.

• Always use a "cliff-hanger," or in other words: don't finish your sentences with a period at the bottom of each page. This makes the prospect want to read what's on the following page. Keep the prospect hanging in anticipation at the end of each page.

• Include a long and unconditional money-back guarantee.

• Use a writing style that is honest and sincere. Skip long, elaborate or technical words. Get the reader nodding in agreement, by stating facts which are blatantly obvious. Use flattery whenever you can. Create a dream scenario. Paint a picture in the prospects mind of him using your product/service. Advise the prospect of what he will miss out on if he doesn't order. Solve the prospects biggest problem or concern. Answer any objections throughout your copy. Tell the prospect "what's in it for him" (as he really is NOT CONCERNED about you or your business).

• Make sure to include a deadline or limited time offer in your sales letter, and highlight this often.

• Sell, sell, sell everywhere in your sales letter. Make sure to end with a call to action.

• Always end with a P.S. in which you summarize your offer one last time. Sign your letter personally or with a different color ink (preferably blue).

• Leave your sales letter alone and come back to it a day later so you can edit it with a clear mind. Use a spell check feature and double-check for grammar mistakes. Have a second set of eyes go over your letter to proofread it.

A brochure. The main reason for including a brochure into your direct mail package is to explain and describe the features of your product or service. It provides proof via photographs, charts, graphs, testimonials and detailed product information. Note that it is possible to accomplish the above in your sales letter, and many direct marketers skip the aspect of the brochure entirely. One of the factors of producing the brochure is its high cost of printing compared to the cheap photocopy costs of your sales letter. This final decision in using a brochure will ultimately be yours. I personally have had excellent success with and without the use of one. A past direct mail package I had created, included only a 4-page sales letter and no brochure, but it had the power to convert 20% of my leads into actual buyers! Such a response rate in direct mail is astronomical! In any event, here are some pointers to assist you in putting together a great brochure:

• Use a folded brochure using a letter or legal sized paper. DO NOT create a booklet or stapled brochure, as this connotes a quality piece indicating to the prospect that he can put it aside and order at his own leisure (something we always want to avoid). Have the brochure professionally designed by using a freelance design student from your nearest community college – the student may even do the work for free to put the brochure in his portfolio. The brochure should fold and fit neatly into your #10 business envelope. Use 4-color printing on both sides, or at the bare minimum 2-color printing. Use lightweight paper to cut down on your mailing costs.

• The outside flap or panel should have a bold headline. The inside of your brochure is where you will do your detailed explaining and this is where you should use sub-heads and short, detailed paragraphs. Use sans serif fonts like "Helvetica," "Optima" or "Arial," as they are easier to read.

• Describe the size, weight, number of pieces in your product, and how it is manufactured. Show photos of people actually using or holding your product. Use graphs, charts, diagrams, technical specifications, or illustrations to describe and show off your product. List all the key features of your product/service.

• Tell your company story by including pictures of you and your staff, pictures of your office, map, address location and full contact information. Write about your background and experience level as the founder of the company.

• Add believable and honest testimonials or lists of past clients. Use photos

of actual clients or users of your product/service. Indicate the name of the client and contact information (if permission is granted) underneath the photos.
• Include a picture of the free gift or premium they get to keep just for ordering your offer.
• Highlight your money-back guarantee again in your brochure, but this time include some kind of a certificate which the prospect can visualize.
• List any back-end customer service or repair service you will provide.
• DO NOT put a time limit on your brochure, as you want to be able to reprint and reuse it over and over again.

A reply form and return envelope. Using a separate reply form (not one that is attached to your brochure or sales letter) will increase results substantially. The reason being is that it is easier for the prospect to respond. He doesn't have to hunt for a pair of scissors to cut out the form or take his time to fold and tear it. A reply form will most likely be a letter sized paper so that you can list all the pertinent requirements, and still have enough space for the prospect to fill it out. Here are some tips on creating your reply form.

• Do not call it an "order" form as this signifies that you are selling to the prospect. Call it a "reply" form or something of similar nature. Design the form in a simple, clear, and easy to fill out layout.
• Under the "reply form" header, add a catchy slogan as to the number of happy prospects that have already used your product. You will not have any customers during your testing phase, but make note of this trick for later on. Write something like this: "Can more than 1,000 satisfied clients be wrong?" People don't want to be the first to try something new, so this will ease some of the buying tension.
• Leave plenty of room for the prospect to fill in his/her return address. Add a small note telling the prospect to "please print" rather than handwrite (which many times is difficult to read and causes undue errors).
• Include all information relating t: method of shipping, time it will take to deliver, applicable taxes, currency being used, quantities of products being ordered. Use rules and columns for ease of filling in quantities, prices and taxes.
• Restate the guarantee and what your return policies are. Make sure to tell the prospect that "no sales people will contact you." This will relieve order anxiety.
• Show a picture of the free gift or promo and describe it one more time.

- Include spaces for credit card information as well as various alternative response methods like: faxing, e-mailing, internet ordering, toll-free phone orders. Include all methods of payment: COD, personal checks, credit cards, money orders, bank drafts.
- State your deadline date when your offer will expire.
- Include a small keyed code somewhere on the form, so that you can track your results if is mailed in.
- Guarantee privacy and discretion in the personal information you will receive, as well as the method of shipment. Reassure the customer that their private information will not be shared with other 3rd parties. Also assure that you will not rent their contact info without their approval.
- Always include a return envelope and stick with a #8 size. It is not necessary to add postage to your return envelope, as studies indicate that this does not increase response.

E-MAIL AND INTERNET MARKETING

E-mail Marketing. There are literally billions of e-mails sent around the world on a daily basis. E-mailing comes with a huge range of advantages over other marketing mediums. Three of the biggest advantages being:

1. It is completely FREE (if you do the e-mailing yourself), there are no postage or shipping costs.
2. The prospects receive your material in a split second, rather than having to wait days to get it via snail mail.
3. There are no printing costs involved to e-mail out your sales material.

Here are some steps to follow, if you would like to try using e-mail as a marketing tool on it's own or to supplement your other campaign activities:

- You can compile your own prospects using directories on the internet which list e-mail addresses and contact information of members.
- You can place small classified ads and direct the responders to leave their e-mail address so that they can receive the "free information package" via e-mail.
- List brokers can send e-mails for you to a specialized group or respondents,

HOW TO CREATE AN UNLIMITED INCOME
SITTING AT HOME IN YOUR PAJAMAS

but it is extremely costly to do this. Brokers will never sell you an e-mail list out right for your own personal use.
• Other marketers advise to get opt-in (or permission) from your prospects before you e-mail them, but if they are responding to your classified ads they will be doing this already by leaving you their e-mail addresses. Compiling your own lists off the internet is another story. Make sure to check with your States laws concerning sending unsolicited e-mails or "spam." Many States understand that a letter cannot be considered spam if the sender includes contact information and a method of removal. So always include an "unsubscribe" feature after your e-mail messages.
• Do your best to always get the prospects permission first, and leave the compiling of unsolicited e-mail addresses as your back-up plan. You can also get people to subscribe for free e-zines or newsletters directly from a web site. By doing so, they click on a button that gives you permission to e-mail them your sales material on an ongoing basis, until they "opt-out" or tell you to stop.

Your next step is to e-mail your sales letter, which is created in the same fashion as if it would be a printed direct mail piece. At the end of your letter, make sure to include your order form so that the prospects can print it out and mail it back, fax it back, or phone in to order.

One interesting thing to remember is that if you are marketing an information product (like a detailed manual or a book), you can have it e-mailed to the prospect in digital format and he can print it out from his end. Zero shipping costs! Zero printing costs! You can actually offer your product at a discount, since you will have very little overhead (practically only advertising costs to generate the leads).

If your product is not an information product, your final step would be to fulfill the order. If you are selling a service, your e-mail promo will probably include a phone number so the prospect can call in for further information or to book the service.

You will notice that with repeated e-mails, your response rate will diminish. What this means is that the first few e-mails that you send to brand new prospects will generate the most sales. Keep the e-mail addresses on your database and manage your own list, removing addresses as requested to do so. Constantly do follow up e-mail promos, perhaps twice a month, but frequency will depend entirely on the product or service you are offering.

Internet Marketing. Marketing on the world wide web has been growing at a phenomenal rate in recent years. If you total the dollars spent each year, as well as the rate of growth, it is quite possible to predict that sales over the internet will reach over billions of dollars per year by the turn of this century. Sure the internet is a fairly new medium to advertise in, but its importance simply cannot be overlooked. I therefore must ask you…if you are a serious direct marketer, how come you are not already building your web site? All joking aside, perhaps we should immediately address this issue with a few stack of pointers and tips:

• Begin right away by picking a suitable domain name which is associated with your company name and checking to see if the domain is still available. If it is, hurry and register it for yourself so as it does not get snapped up by someone else.

• Hire a community college design student to create a web site for you (if you are not tech savvy). As mentioned earlier, these students are hungry for actual-world portfolio samples (rather than classroom projects), and you may be able to negotiate a small web site for free.

• Make sure to create your site with easily loading graphics, and skip the loud music and animations if these do not correspond with your target market. If your idea is focused to CEO's of companies, then you should not use funky audio or graphics.

• Add pertinent and valuable information on your site, so as your potential prospects will come back to your site frequently to look for new material. Update your site often with fresh ideas and content.

• A navigation bar on each page should be included, as well as a site map for your site.

• Create a company story page that includes a photo of yourself and your staff.

• Include metatags (key codes) in the software codes so the search engines will have an easy time picking up keyword searches and posting your web site high on the rankings. A web master can assist you with writing the codes. Take extra care when creating the key words for submissions. Use the maximum amount allowed by each search engine. Be sure to use plural versions, as well as commonly misspelled versions of your key words.

• For quick and top placement of your site, use paid submission companies (you pay per use or per click). Go to the major search engines and they should have a link about how to go about submitting your web site. Try to avoid the free search engines, as they take a very long time to get your site listed, and when you do get listed in all likelihood you will not have a top ranking spot. If your goal is to create a professional site for the purposes of generating business income, then go with the paid-per-click route.

• Incorporate a complete contact page on your site, which lists your address, fax number, telephone numbers and a direct link to your e-mail address.

• Build free items on your site, anything from: newsletters, e-zines (electronic magazines), audio clips, video clips. Ultimately, try to get as many mailing addresses and e-mail addresses from your visitors so you can begin an aggressive marketing campaign on them.

• Post your web site address onto all your other marketing and company materials like your: business cards, stationary, faxes, brochures, sales letters, ads, invoices, etc. This will generate extra traffic to your site.

• The real payday will be apparent when you begin:
listing your web site with other web masters,
start using free links,
start swapping links,
using message boards,
joining discussion forums,
joining newsgroups,
getting into banner exchange programs.
All the proceeding tips will increase your site traffic tremendously.

• Purchase and implement an auto-respond system. Auto-responders automatically send e-mails to prospects who order from you, contact you, or ask for further information. The messages you send are easily editable, trackable (you can check to see who read your e-mails), and you can even add an "unsubscribe" link at the end of your messages. You can stay connected with your present or future clients within seconds and without you being present, which makes auto-responders an integral item in your marketing arsenal.

• Use paid submission companies to submit your site to the search engines, they are of far superior quality than free submission services.

• Endorse someone else's site which is somehow related to your product or service, and get that other company to endorse your site in return.

• Keep in touch with your visitors on a consistent basis to ask about problems and concerns and ways to improve your site. Create a board room or chat room to discuss issues, complaints and their resolutions.

• Do a search on the internet for "Free Advertising" and without a doubt, you will be amazed at what pops up. Make it a habit to spend at least an hour

a day adding yourself to free advertising companies.
 • Check your stats page to see how many visitors you get on a daily basis so you can measure your internet marketing success.
 • Be careful about adding too many exit links onto your site. You want your prospects to have enough time to surf your site and possibly place an order, before they link to another web site and never return.
 • Use the direct mail section (earlier in this chapter), to add powerful copy content on your web site. Since it is so quick and easy to post anything on the internet, most of the content which is being produced is of the lowest quality. Don't follow the masses by adding fluff to your site. Add only the most empowering content that you can create, and this will attract and keep visitors coming back to your site.
 • Create a "bookmark us" button on your web site so visitors can save your homepage on their computers for easy retrieval later.
 • Add a client list page or a testimonial page and show photos of your past and present happy customers. This will help build trust and credibility to your site.
 • As most searchers do not bother to check following pages after they do a key word search, make it your goal to be ranked on the first page of the top 10 search engines. And although it is quite time-consuming to submit yourself over and over again to search engines, there are companies and software available that can do this for you. Do a search for "web positioning software" and see what you find.
 • Make sure to edit your site for spelling and grammar mistakes. Make sure to surf around yourself so as to identify any bugs which need correcting. Also test your site in various web browsers for proof that your site will be seen as you expect it to. Get friends and family to surf around on a test version of your site, before you actually post it on the internet. Then you can send out your Grand Opening notices!

FAX BROADCASTING

Due to the fact that nearly all businesses have a fax machine, fax marketing is a cost-effective method of implementing a business-to-business direct response campaign. You can compile your own fax list by using directories or associations over the internet. Build your list by entering the fax numbers into a program such as Excel. If you can compile a listing of 1,000 fax numbers, this should be sufficient in doing an initial testing.

Fax broadcasting companies will send out the faxes for you at a minimal cost. Usually these companies charge a per-page fee as well as any long-distance phone charges, if applicable. Using a fax broadcast company will save you both time and money. I made the error of paying an in-house fax person, before I got on the bandwagon of using fax broadcasting companies.

If you compile your own fax numbers and use a fax broadcasting company, expect to pay in the range of about 10 cents per page. If you can, try to compile your first group of fax numbers in your local area so you don't have to pay for long distance charges. In this fashion, you may be able to do a testing of your offer to 1,000 prospects for approximately $100.

Aside from the low costs involved in delivering your offer, also note that you have no printing costs. You also do not have to stuff envelopes, fold your sales material, and apply postage. The delivery method is instantaneous (sometimes within a couple of hours). Alternatively, with a direct mail campaign you will have to wait up to a week for your offer to reach your prospect. All these advantages combined make fax broadcasting an essential marketing tool.

When creating your fax promo, please adhere to the direct mail advice in writing your promo. The headline, again, will be of major importance. I try to keep my fax promotions to one page, or as short as possible. The reason for this is that faxing is the only direct marketing tool which shifts the cost of the promotion directly to the prospect. Basically, you use up the prospect's paper and ink when you fax to them. You will notice that many prospects will not take to this too well, and you may get a backlash of phone calls (sometimes from irate callers) informing you to remove them from your fax list.

By the same token, the Federal Communication Committee passed a law back in 1992 cracking down on unsolicited fax campaigns. In fact, I believe the penalty can be as steep as $500 PER PAGE THAT YOU SEND. Therefore, I ask you to check with your area's laws prior to doing a fax promo, and be aware of the consequences. A common rule when sending unsolicited faxes is to include your contact address, your fax number, as well as a method for the prospects to remove their number from your database. You may be required to manage your own list of contacts, or your fax broadcasting company may be able to do this for you for a small monthly fee.

In conclusion, fax marketing is an excellent add-on marketing tool to supplement your classified ad or direct marketing campaigns. Without a doubt, you will definitely receive extra leads using the fax marketing method, but you will also ruffle a few feathers in the process.

DELIVERY OF PRINTED MATERIAL DOOR-TO-DOOR

Subsequently, due again to the low costs in both production and distribution methods, door-to-door marketing is another profitable area you should not overlook. Hiring local high school students or using a distribution company will both be a suitable method of delivery. There are a number of door-to-door products that you can concentrate your energies on:

Door Hangers. As the name details, a door hanger is shaped to hang on the door handle of main entrance doors. The attractive advantage of this is that your marketing message is not lost in a crowded mailbox along with other marketing pieces and unpaid bills. When your prospect returns home, he will find your door hanger right where he will be inserting his key or placing his hand. What a fantastic way of reaching your prospect directly and without any other competition!

You will find that door hangers are extremely affordable to print. Do a search for companies in your local Yellow Pages Directory for companies that create them and print them. It is imperative to use the best weight of paper possible, and opt for 4-color hangers over 2-color or black. Again, your main focus is to get the prospects attention, and hit them with an interesting and irresistible offer.

I have used door hangers for many years now with surprising results. Depending on your offer, you can expect a 2 – 5% response rate, so if you have 1,000 hangers delivered, you may receive 50 calls. Door hangers work well when your business is focused to a mass market. Ideally, service businesses will do extremely well by using this marketing method. Taking the time to do initial market research for the required demographics of a certain locality, will also increase your response rate for the type of business you are marketing.

Flyers. Another low cost marketing tool! Flyers (or circulars) can be printed for pennies each and again the distribution costs are minimal. Keep your flyer to letter size and use only one color so that you can photocopy it in black. You may want to experiment with a different color paper rather than just white. Some of the fluorescent papers are quite eye-catching! Flyers can be delivered door-to-door by using hungry high school students as freelance employees. You can also deliver them to: mall parking lots, Laundromats, telephone poles, transit waiting areas, windshields of cars, outside of large sports stadiums, inside daily or weekly newspapers as an insert, and in business

*HOW TO CREATE AN UNLIMITED INCOME
SITTING AT HOME IN YOUR PAJAMAS*

storefronts (ask permission from the owners first).

Flyers can also be created into point of purchase displays by mounting them onto foamboard or foamcore and creating an easel. Curiously, 75% of retail sales are impulse buys…so I can't think of a better way to get your product in front of the waiting eyes of retail buyers. If your new idea is a product, you can negotiate with retailers (with some sort of paid incentive) to allow you to put up your display in their retail stores. The owners should be warm to an offer such as this, after all, this will generate some extra income for the store. The offer will be even tastier if it is of no risk to the owner – or on a consignment basis.

Card Deck Inserts, Credit Card Inserts and Mail Box Inserts. Three more door-to-door delivery methods with their low cost printing and distribution methods. Card desks can cost around five cents each as compared to a direct mail campaign which can cost around one dollar each for printing, supplies and stuffing of the envelopes. A wide array of business can use card decks to present their offering.

Similarly, credit card inserts are a low cost way to reach a target market. They piggy-back along with a prospects credit card statement. And naturally, the prospects are able to afford your offer since their credit is good enough to qualify for a credit card.

Mail box inserts are a collaboration of mostly service businesses, who gang up together in one plastic bag or envelope and get delivered door-to-door. This marketing method is ideal for service business who want to target a specific area in their surrounding sales region. Most companies that coordinate and handle the delivery of inserts can assist with demographics selections categorized by postal or zip codes. One obvious disadvantage with mail box inserts as that the package is usually crowded with many other offers and your prospect is bombarded with messages as soon as the package is opened. You have to really offer a superb discount and coupon to get the prospect to take action.

I do not believe that the above mentioned inserts can stand alone to generate the sufficient leads you will need to test your idea. Use them as a secondary back-up to a direct mail, classified ads or computer marketing campaign.

TELEMARKETING

Here is an interesting fact: If you do any sort of direct mail, e-mail, or fax marketing and then following up with a phone call, you can increase your sales rate by 20 – 30%. Isn't that incredible? Think about it for a minute. How many times have you received an interesting direct mail piece in which you thought "hey this sounds like a great deal I think I will call them" but then you put it aside and forget about it? It happens all the time. Now imagine getting called and reminded about that direct mail piece. Don't you think that this simple action would generate an increased response? It sure would.

By the same token, many times prospects will have questions and inquiries about your direct mail, ad, etc. but will be too shy or scared to call you. Take the initiative and phone them instead.

Make it a habit to follow up all your other marketing campaigns with a telemarketing program. Here are some things that I have learned about telemarketing through my experiences:

• The first thing to never forget is that when ever you phone anyone you are actually disturbing their present situation (they may have been doing chores, spending quality time with their family, etc) and so you must at all times be courteous and show respect.

• Don't make cold calls. Wait until you have interested leads that have contacted you, or prospects that you have sent your sales material to in the past. Warm prospects will have some sort of inclination of who you are and will often show a better response to your offer.

• Don't use a script. Know what the main theme of your call is and work around that. This way you will not sound like a salesman trying to make his pitch.

• Make sure you have the proper person on the line who can make the final decision about purchasing your product/service.

• Don't start off with a "Good morning, Mr. John Smith, my name is Rose from so and so company." This will get the prospects "telemarketing warning flag" rising. Be casual but professional, start off with something simple like "Hi John, how are you today?" Then when John asks, you can tell him which company you're calling from.

• Talk at a normal rate, not too fast or too slow. Too fast and you will sound like a "used car salesman," too slow and you will bore them to death!

• You have 20 seconds to grab the prospect's attention or you have lost them, and they will mentally shut down on you. Make your most important, colossal benefit very early in your first few sentences.

• Don't try to sell a product/service over the phone that requires some sort of difficult introduction, presentation, or detailed technical guidance, as it will not work. Basically if your idea has to be sold in person, then do the selling in person (have the prospect come to your home).

CREATING AN INBOUND CALL CENTER

Your direct response marketing campaign will generate may interested prospects. These prospects will start calling you for further information or to place orders for your brilliant new idea. You have to be prepared and well organized to take these calls.

One of the most important items to remember is you have to be available for your customers when they do call. If you are going to be operating a service business geared to homeowners, you will soon find out that many people wait until they come home from work to make their phone calls. If you are selling to business people, then probably 9 – 5 hours will suffice. Keep in mind that if you have clients in the East or West Coast they will be operating at different time zones and will be calling at odd hours of the day. Some people who shop via the internet or through mail order do so in the late evenings or on the weekends. Make sure that you can accommodate all your prospects.

If you are selling very high priced items and getting one or two orders a day, then of course hiring a full time sales staff will not be necessary. But what happens if you introduce a hot product to the market place and you are receiving 300 calls a day? You will have to scramble to hire talented phone reps to take the calls. Phone calls will have to be answered in a timely manner. Not letting prospects hear a busy signal will be another problem which you will have to contend with. In fact, an interesting marketing idea is to run an "on-hold discount promotion." Instead of listening to elevator music, on hold prospects can listen to a pre-recorded message along the lines of "we appreciate your patience and today's on-hold discount is 5% off any orders over $200, please mention the discount to your phone rep."

If you do have to hire staff to take inbound calls, one very important question they must get in the habit of asking is "Which newspaper are you calling from?" or "How did you hear about us?" This is one of the best methods of finding out exactly which advertising medium is producing the highest response for you.

Additionally, be aware of the type of staff that should be hired and the main responsibilities that they will have to perform. If the bulk of your incoming calls will be writing down orders, booking appointments or taking payment/address information, then you will not have to hire a "professional closer" of a salesperson. But if your product or service will require some extra hand-holding, advice, or suggestions, then it will be to your benefit to hire a more professional sales rep. Because of their increased responsibility and client contact, top-closing sales reps have to be fully trained. They should know your products/services like the back of their hands!

INVENTING YOUR OWN STRATEGIC MARKETING CAMPAIGNS

You should now have the information and understanding to begin designing a marketing campaign to test the demand your product will generate when offered to the general public. Based on your budget, and how much of the work you plan to do yourself, there are literally an endless number of campaigns that you can create. By inventing groupings of: the way you generate your leads, the method you receive those leads, and the fulfillment method to deliver the goods, you are basically tailoring a campaign that fits your needs perfectly. Keep in mind, that at this point, all you are trying to accomplish is to see if your target market will take a bite at your offer. You are gauging the **DEMAND OF THE MARKET**. In essence you are reaching out to touch your prospects, in the hopes that they return the favor by giving you their cash. Forgo any thoughts of actually fulfilling your product or service, we will discuss this in the next chapter. However, you can start planning the fulfillment method you will want to use later on.

The examples following are for illustrative purposes only, and you may modify them as you see fit. I will show you just a few of the endless possibilities that are available, when inventing your own Strategic Marketing Campaigns:

• Compile a list of contacts off the internet, send them a direct mail package, they phone in and speak to a live salesperson who books an appointment and makes a proposal, you e-mail out the written proposal, you follow up with a telemarketing campaign.

• Place classified ads, prospects call in and speak to a live salesperson who books a free service evaluation and quote. Your trained staff do the running around and close the sales for you.

HOW TO CREATE AN UNLIMITED INCOME
SITTING AT HOME IN YOUR PAJAMAS

• Place classified ads, prospects listen to a free recorded message and leave their addresses, you mail them a direct mail package, they mail you out their payment. No person-to-person contact is involved with this method.

• You compile a list of contacts off the internet, send them an e-mail promo. They e-mail you back their payment information. Total financial outlay = zero.

• You use your web site traffic to generate contact information, you mail out your direct mail package, prospects call in to place an order. Others fax back or mail in their orders.

• You place classified ads, prospects call in and are greeted by a professional sales rep who sells them immediately over the phone, you ship their product out COD.

• You deliver door hangers door-to-door, prospects call in and speak to a live customer service rep who books a free demonstration.

• You compile a list of fax numbers off of an internet directory, you contact a fax broadcasting company and send out a fax promo, customers call in and ask for their free kit, you mail out the kit, you follow up with a telemarketing campaign.

• You find a list of e-mail addresses from an association over the internet, you send prospects an e-mail promo, they e-mail you back requesting your free special reports, you e-mail the reports to the prospects.

• You compile a list of fax numbers off the internet from prospects in your local area, you fax out a promo yourself, contacts call in to place an order, you handle the calls and do the selling personally. Total financial outlay = zero.

• Using your web site traffic you generate an e-mail list from prospects who "opt-in" to receive free information, you e-mail out a newsletter on a monthly basis, prospects buy your product over the internet from your web site. This can be a totally automated marketing campaign.

Chapter 4
Positioning for Solid Growth and Showing a Profit

This chapter is all about the systems, strategies and ideas which will teach you how to build a solid direct marketing business and position it for future growth. You will learn about management, fulfillment, employees, knowing when to abandon an idea, correcting advertising mistakes, and most importantly **SHOWING A PROFIT**. The type of desired profit will also be revealed and discussed in detail. After all, business is all about selling something to someone, and reaping a handsome profit in the end. Ultimately, the bottom line will be the most important number. So without further ado, let's begin the next chapter in our exciting voyage together.

YOU WILL FAIL 7 TIMES OUT OF 10 TRIES!

This should be an eye-opening statement for most direct marketing beginners. Provided you know of the odds and are expecting them, then you will have a greater chance of hanging in for the long haul. So let it sink in. Out of 10 business ideas that you concoct and bring to market, 7 of them will be total failures. They will not generate a high demand, and they will only cause you to show a small loss on your balance statement. Two out of ten ideas will show a measly profit, but not enough of a profit for you to spend considerable amounts of time trying to revive them into a full-blown successful venture. Only 1 out of 10 of your ideas will be a hands-down winner. Such a winner will be capable of being fertilized, pruned, and matured into a majestic money-tree!

HOW TO KNOW WHEN YOU HAVE A WINNER

There is a mathematical formula that I use to identify my winners. It goes like this:

The Cost Per Order + Complete Cost of your product/service = 100% return on your advertising investment

Remember how we discussed wealth-building rates of return in Chapter One? This is finally where we begin to see it being applied for our own benefits. To simplify the above mathematical formula I will put it in these words: If you total the advertising cost per order and the complete cost of your idea, you should end up getting a 100% return on your invested capital. So if I spend $100, I should end up with $200 in my pocket. Wow…you must be thinking these rates of return are incredible, but do I really need them that high? Of course you do! If you are interested in joining the masses and earning 3% by buying bank products, go right ahead. If you are interested in creating a financially free lifestyle then shoot for a 100% return on your direct marketing investments. Anything short of this should be unacceptable.

I will give you examples from two of my businesses so that you can visualize that these rates of returns are feasible and possible. In my marketing/advertising business I spend approximately $1,000 per month on advertising expenses which bring back over $20,000 on a monthly basis. This is a 2,000% monthly return on my invested dollars. In one of my other service-oriented companies, I spend $1,000 per month on advertising, which returns me an income of $8,000 (700% monthly growth).

Another observable fact is that your advertising budget will be your largest expenditure in direct marketing. And taking into account the 100% return that we will be shooting for, then it is easy to see that your advertising costs will be approximately 50% of your total expenses. So therefore, be willing to expect and budget for: **50% of your income to be spent on advertising**

This might seem inordinately high for any other type of business, where 10 to 20% is the norm. But this is the direct response business, folks. We have to get the word out and educate the public about our ideas. This takes money. This takes more money than other ordinary mainstream businesses.

SO YOU DON'T HAVE A WINNER OR A LOSER

As we mentioned above, 2 out of 10 times you will receive some sort of positive feedback from your initial tests. You may spend $50 on classified ads in one week, and you may end up making $60 in return (or a measly $10 profit). Now the question remains, do you want to throw your whole energies into placing more ads when your profit margin is so low? By expanding and placing more ads, say $1,000 worth of ads in one week, you will end up making $1,200—or a $200 profit. Hardly worth the extra effort, don't you agree?

I can't advise you at this point to dump the idea which is producing mediocre returns. Once in a while, a mediocre return can be molded into a solid money-maker by testing, re-testing and changing the variables of your offer. Often, though, the work involved to make the necessary changes is so time-consuming, that it is hardly worth the effort trying. Why kill yourself to make an extra $500 profit a week, for example, when a hit of an idea will be making you $2,000 a day? I have personally made this error (a few times in fact), trudging along, trying to "wake a dead dog by beating it with a stick," all to no avail. All I ended up doing was wasting a whole year of my precious time! Save your time and invest your energy only on your outright winners. That is my recommendation.

PERFECTING YOUR MARKETING CAMPAIGNS

Sometimes total outright failures are a result of a poor marketing campaign, and not related at all to the quality of your idea. The direct response business requires the creative grouping of a whole fist-full of variables, which all have to be working together nicely, to turn your idea into a success. You need a strong offer, a great headline, an unconditional money-back guarantee, a reasonable price, a good economic climate, little or no competition, etc. etc. Do you see what I mean? If you do get a failure, or a near miss, it can only mean that either your idea is a flop or your marketing campaign is.

Now supposing you placed some test classified ads and your phone starts ringing off the hook. That's fabulous news! But you send out your sales

HOW TO CREATE AN UNLIMITED INCOME
SITTING AT HOME IN YOUR PAJAMAS

material and you receive zero orders. This is a clear indication that there is a demand for your idea, that your prospects were highly accepting of your offer. The problem lies with your sales package, as it did not do its job in closing the sales. Well, half the battle has been won, all you have to do is revamp your sales package and you will be taking your mail order checks straight to the bank!

Following are some reasons why your ad campaign may be failing. Look at these carefully to see if they relate to your campaign, and if you can modify and correct your mistakes in the future.

- The economic climate may be off (there may be a recession, or high unemployment)
- You could be advertising at the wrong time of the year
- You might be advertising in the wrong type of newspaper or other medium
- You might not have picked your target market properly
- Your idea does not satisfy one of the basic human desires
- Too much competition exists for your idea category
- The market is already too saturated with your type of product/service
- The headline of your ads or sales literature is not powerful enough
- You advertised in the wrong heading of the newspaper
- The price of your product/service is not right (too high or too low)
- Your sales letter itself is not strong enough
- Your brochure is not designed professionally and gives a cheap appearance
- The body copy of your ads or sales package does not create interest
- You are not selling with benefits, but are concentrating too much on the features
- You did not use strong testimonials (more on this shortly)
- Your offer does not come across as believable and honest

A slight change in one or some of the above components may produce a measurable outcome in your marketing campaign. Even a one word change in a headline, for example, has been known to pull in 300% more leads! Think of yourself as a mad scientist who is trying to invent the next revolutionary product. All you have to do is combine the right dash or this, the right sprinkle of that, and you will uncover a runaway hit of an idea. Just be persistent and keep testing, changing and combining the various components.

DUMP THE DOGS AND FLY WITH YOUR WINNERS

Without a doubt, one of the most mind-draining experiences in the direct response business is becoming too emotionally attached with one of your crazy ideas. After closely studying and constant changing of the above variables, does not produce a winner…then let the dead dog lie! How much time and energy you want to invest into each idea will be your own personal decision. I cannot give you a deadline here. There are just too many variables involved, too many goals and too many values. Just know that you must be prepared to sever the ties to many of your idea "dogs." Most of your ideas will be beyond rescue, so save your money, time, and energy for other worthwhile projects.

Let me tell you the joy that you will experience when you have a hands-down winner right at the start of an advertising campaign! It is a feeling like nothing else in the world! Not only will there be an astronomical demand from the public, but you will be closing sales so fast that you will have a difficult time fulfilling your product or service. This is the position that will make up for all the losers you invented earlier. The profits from a winner such as this will assist you in recouping all the losses from your previous "dead dogs" many times over. So when you get lucky and produce a winner right from the start, run with it for as long as you can!

SPLIT TESTING

Commonly called the "A/B Test," split testing is the process of testing two different factors against each other to see which produces the better results. It doesn't necessarily have to be split in two, either. You can do an A/B/C test – or split it in three. Or an A/B/C/D test, and split it in four. So how do you go about doing a simple split test? Let's say for example that you have placed a classified ad which has resulted in 1,000 leads. You might be at the beginning of introducing your idea to the market place, so you will be eager in establishing the right price of your idea. What you would do is send 500 offers at one price and then 500 offers with a completely different price. **Note: that for your split test to be correct, you should only test one element in your offer each time you do a test. All the other elements must remain identical**. What elements can you test? You can test:

*HOW TO CREATE AN UNLIMITED INCOME
SITTING AT HOME IN YOUR PAJAMAS*

Headlines
The Price
Your Complete Offer
The List
Guarantees

These are the standard elements to test against each other. You can also test things like free gifts, including a brochure or not, alternate reply elements, etc.

But let's get back to pricing for a minute. You have a hot new product and you want to find the right price to sell it at in the marketplace. If you have 1,000 leads to mail to, you may want to do an A/B/C test where you mail 333 leads one price (say $150), the next 333 leads at $200, the final 333 leads a price of $250. Then you track your responses and find out which price brought you in the most sales. You will be surprised to uncover that many times the higher price is the one that will pull in the most orders. Why? Because the prospect believes that the higher price is an indication of "higher perceived value," basically the prospect thinks you are offering a valuable product if the price is high.

You can test the price in your initial 1,000 mailing, then you might want to test the headline in your next mailing. I repeat: test only one element each time you do a mailing. Furthermore, make sure to test to the same group of leads for valid results. You might get different results if you test the exact same offering to two different lists.

Additionally, if you decide you want to purchase a mailing list of 10,000 prospects, it might be wise to only purchase a list of 1,000 names from that list, and test to them first. The response you get will tell you whether the remaining 9,000 names are going to be a profitable buy. **In fact, scientific testing has revealed that you can test to 1/10 of a list and expect to achieve pinpoint accurate results with the remaining of the names on the list.** What this means is, if you do a test to 2,000 prospects on a list, you can safely test up to a total of 20,000 names from the same list and still achieve the same results.

DON'T DO TRIVIAL TESTS

Be careful on testing small and trivial elements. You wouldn't want to test three different prices in this way: $150, $160, $170, as the results you gather will not really be worthwhile. Make sure to test only the factors that will be of major importance to your marketing campaign. The two most important elements are usually: The Price and the Offer.

KEEP TESTING

Make it a habit to be constantly testing every mailing or offer you send out. Use the results you get, for the consistent polishing of your direct response campaign. Even if a product offering is highly successful, keep testing to see if you can improve it in any way. Do not make assumptions as to what will bring in the best results. Many times what you expect to work, will turn out to be a dismal failure. Other times a slight modification in your testing, will produce a colossal financial result. Don't second-guess your prospects. Throw your ideas into the marketplace, test them consistently, and your prospects actions will give you the answers that are required for your success.

TRACKING YOUR RESULTS

You will have to implement some sort of system for tracking the results of your tests. You have to know where each reply came from. Was it from this list? Or was it from that ad? Or could it be from that direct mail campaign? Here are some ways to track your different advertising mediums and various campaigns:

• Put a small code on the reply element of your direct mail package or in your print ads. It could be: dept. A0915 (identifying that this is an order from the direct mail piece that you mailed out on September 15). The letter before the number will reveal that this is group "A" as opposed to group "B."
• Ask the prospects from one medium to call in and ask for a certain person: Joe Smith, ask prospects from another medium to ask for: Jane Doe. Make up imaginary staff members that don't really exist…they are only mentioned for tracking purposes.
• Get your customer service staff that answers the calls, to ask: "Where are you calling from?" or "Which ad are you calling from?" or "How did you hear about us?"
• You can place only one ad from each area code, so that when prospects

call in you will know by the area code which area they are calling from.
• Tell callers to ask for a certain extension when they phone in to place an order. This extension will be the tracking code.
• Use a different "keeper gift," a different "discount amount," or a different "free offer" in each mailing that you do.

THE CUSTOMER'S LIFETIME VALUE & ADDITIONAL PRODUCT OFFERINGS

This is perhaps one of the top ten most important points to remember in the direct response business. It is widely known that when a new customer purchases your product or service, this represents only 5% of the total volume of sales you will eventually receive from this client, if you retain him for the long term. If your client pays you $50 for an initial product, he will most likely end up investing $1,000 in further products during your mutual business relationship. This is why it is imperative to create **back-end products** (or a diversified product line) as fast as you can. Now you know how CD and video mail order houses can afford to sell five of their initial products for pennies on the dollar—because they know that they will make a handsome profit down the road with their back-end sales. Therefore, take mental note of this: **It is customary practice in mail order to break even or lose money on initial sales.**

My thoughts about quick sales and back-end products is this: **Try to make as much profit as you can, as quickly as you possibly can.** I believe in instant and profitable returns. I don't want to wait two years to make a profit, do you? Besides, the abovementioned mail order houses have huge budgets and investor backing. They can afford to wait to rake in their profits. But you are a little guy in the mail order arena. You should be scouting for the quick buck ideas. You are looking for ideas that you can test fast and cheap. Don't get me wrong, I don't disagree with having back-end products, I think they are just as important in the whole scheme of things. **Back-end products should be used to supplement your income and give you a solid base of residual finances.**

One way to use back-end products in a clever way is to include a company catalogue or second product offering with the first product that a client orders. This way, he may be extremely interested in the second offering and place an order immediately. This is called a **"bounce-back order."** As well, there is a strategy in which your prospect orders a product from you and you contact the prospect a short time later to offer a much higher-priced **"upgraded product."** You should allow the prospect to return the first item and reduce this product's price from the upgraded product. Another strategy is to place an ad for one product and when the prospect calls in to order, you advise him of **"add-on products"** (like carrying cases, accessories, extra attachments, etc.) which he can purchase. This strategy can also work well with service businesses, for example: when your service technician is in the home performing the agreed work, he can "up sell" more expensive additional services.

Another surprising source of income that bears mentioning here, is something called **"drag."** These are the extra orders that trickle in after you have stopped your advertising campaign. From every direct response promo that you do, there will be a small fragment of the prospects who will put your offer aside and will eventually place an order—sometime in the distant future! They may order two or three months after your initial offering. Once in a while they misplace your offer, only to find it six months later and place an order. Drag is a funny, but nevertheless, much appreciated phenomenon!

ELIMINATING FREE-LOADERS

For certain ideas that you will be marketing, you will notice that your offering will attract an extremely high number of "Free-Loaders," candidates who are just out to get free products and have no inclination to buy your product/service. Perhaps you have seen individuals such as this walking around malls tasting free samples, or at trade shows packing their bags full of free brochures. Our goal as direct marketers is to generate as much hype and interest as we can, but still put some sort of "weeding out system" in force, to get rid of prospects that are not qualified to purchase our product or service.

Here are some tips to assist you:

- Skim the crowd for the cream of the crop. The upper-end, high-income earners.
- Make them pay for the postage on return envelopes.
- Make them pay for the long distance call – don't use a toll-free line.
- Let them pay for any initial product promotions – don't offer them for free.

- Market only to extremely targeted, niche-driven prospects.
- Put them through a stringent pre-qualification system of calls, forms, or appointments that they must complete before they can receive your full information.

Again I repeat that only certain offers will attract a large amount of "free loaders" and you must be ready and prepared to put the above tips in place to weed them out—before they suck you dry!

PRE-QUALIFYING LEADS

Quite often when dealing with potential prospects, we get unexpectedly thrown some kind of monkey-wrench out of the blue, and it hits us like a ton of bricks! We wonder where in the world did that come from? If only I could have uncovered that, right at the beginning of the sales process, I could have saved so much wasted time. Well here are a few obstacles that you should be aware of, so that you can tackle them head on right from the start.

• When does the prospect want the product delivered or installed? Usually the prospects that want it the quickest are the better prospect. Others that put it off usually don't stick to their agreed upon delivery date, and eventually cancel their order.

• Can the prospect afford what I have to sell? Do they have the right down payment, the good credit, the high income needed? This is definitely a deal-breaker, try to find out the affordability issue as soon as you can.

• Do they truly need what I have to offer...or is it just a passing whim? Do they have something similar now? How can my product/service assist them by improving their lives?

• Are they the one who will make the final decision? Sometimes both a wife and husband should be sold at the same time. In business–to–business sales there are usually many levels of the approval stage which have to be unraveled.

• Watch out for other miscellaneous deal-breakers like: Does the prospect have any issues that will take precedence over his decision to purchase my product? Like perhaps his car's engine just blew up, and he needs his funds to buy a new engine. Does my product require a certain license or educational background that the prospect does not have? Is the prospect in an area of the country that we do not service, or in an area that we cannot ship to?

IDEA LIFE CYCLE

Every product category has a birthing stage, a growing stage and a dying stage. You should be keenly aware of the stage that your product fits in at the present moment, so that you can market it accordingly. Whether you are promoting a service, a product or an idea, it doesn't really matter. Each category will go through the same stages. Let's go through the stages one at a time and see what sort of strategic marketing systems you will have to employ to stay alive.

Birthing Stage. This is where you contrive your idea and it takes shape. You bring your product to market. In this stage you have to educate your end users about your new product. Depending on how revolutionary your idea is, this may require a lot of funds and a lot of patience on your part. Especially if your new idea requires mass change from what the population is used to, expect to receive quite a bit of opposition. Your main goal will be opening up various sales markets as fast as you can. Gaining market dominance should also be a main priority. By giving out free or discounted samples, you can gain access to a large market share.

Growing Stage. In this stage the growth is outstanding. Competitors come out of the woodwork to grab a piece of the pie. Your prospects are using your product, and market sales are approximately 15% of the total available sales for the product category. Because of the wide-open territory, all competitors are happy, as they are all making a tidy profit. During this phase, you are concerned with growing your brand's awareness, grabbing as big a market share as you can, and improving your product to make it the best. Fighting off the competition as it nips you in the behind will obviously be another big priority.

Dying Stage. Now the market has been saturated. Everyone owns one of your products, or one of your competitor's. People stop buying new products and start replacing their older models with better quality upgraded versions. In this final stage, your main concern will be stealing customers from your competitors. New customers won't exist. You will have to do your best to hang onto the customers that you do have, as it will be easier to sell to them rather than try to find new ones. You will be focused on increasing the quality, speed and durability of your product/service. You will also be heavy into experimenting on ways to improve your basic models with upgraded versions and different models.

BE AWARE OF THE ITCH CYCLE

Knowing as much as you can about your prospects has a set of distinct advantages. One of these advantages is understanding that all products and services have a limited time span. They get used up and then get re-ordered. Sometimes they get replaced just because the person using them has gotten bored or wants a better, upgraded model. That is what an itch cycle is—the prospect is getting "itchy" and he needs to get "scratched." Now imagine the buckets of money you can make if you could identify when every prospects "itch cycle" was going to take place? For instance, if you were selling moving services and you learned that the average homeowner moves every 7 years? Well I hope you would do an aggressive marketing campaign to these homeowners during their sixth year to try and grab their upcoming business! If the average car owner replaces his car every 4 years, you would be marketing like gang-busters in their third year of ownership, wouldn't you?

How does this relate to a beginning direct response student such as yourself? It builds awareness. It let's you know that you should begin organizing an itch cycle database as soon as possible. Here are the proper steps to take in sequence:

- Locate a computer database program and put it to use
- Record the date of each sale that you make
- Record the amount of money that the customer spent
- Research to identify what the itch cycle is for your product/service category
- Keep your database lean, current and accurate
- Advertise like a maniac to your present customers right before their itch cycles!

LEGALITIES INVOLVED WITH MAIL ORDER

Organizing yourself on a solid foundation in this business, means knowing your legal obligations and requirements as a mail order operator. There is so much money available to be made in a legal and ethical fashion (especially in direct response), that I am amazed at the number of people that are swayed into taking the illegal route. Unfortunately, you may by accident market a product that carries with it a stiff fine or worse – a lengthy prison sentence! I'll highlight a list of the most common illegalities which you may unknowingly get involved with:

1. **Any scheme which involves swindling the public in any way**
2. **Unlawful lottery or pyramid schemes**
3. **Betting, wagering, or bookmaking**
4. **Obscene, pornographic, or indecent material**
5. **Any message sent with intent to obtain funds under false pretences**

PROHIBITED ITEMS

Doing business in Canada, I am fully aware of the legalities surrounding our Canadian Provinces. I will list these as cautionary items only—these may or may not be illegal in your area—SO I ADVISE YOU TO CHECK WITH YOUR COUNTRY'S LAWS. Prohibited items are defined as any item which is prohibited by law, or which contains products or substances that could harm Canada Post Corporation employees, soil or damage postal equipment and other shipments.

The following is a partial list of prohibited items:
- Intoxicating beverages, except when shipped by provincial liquor boards/commissions or shipped by manufacturers of such beverages to provincial liquor boards/commissions or between any of them, or when shipped from a provincial liquor board/commission to any person, or when shipped by provincial liquor board/commission to foreign manufacturers or distributors of intoxicating beverages.
- Narcotics, as defined in the Narcotics Control Act or the regulations made pursuant of that Act.

*HOW TO CREATE AN UNLIMITED INCOME
SITTING AT HOME IN YOUR PAJAMAS*

- Controlled drugs and restricted drugs, as defined in the Food and Drug Act or the regulations made pursuant of that Act.
- Samples of drugs unless addressed to doctors, dentists, veterinary surgeons or registered pharmacists, in accordance with the Food and Drug Act regulations.
- Any article emitting an offensive or noxious odor.
- Liquids, oils, fatty substances, fish, game, meat, fresh fruit, vegetables and other perishable items that are not prepared in accordance with Canada Post Corporation standards.
- Human or animal blood, unless packaged in accordance with the conditions and requirements specified by Canada Post Corporation standards.

Animals, Birds, Insects, etc. Generally, living creatures are not acceptable for shipping because of health, humane treatment, handling and transportation feasibility, and related cost considerations. However, pursuant to an agreement with Canada Post, exceptions can be made providing specific conditions are met (example: for bees, day-old chicks, parasites, and destroyers intended for noxious insects).

Dead birds, animals or their parts are acceptable only when the cover of the package bears a full description of the contents; the name and address of the shipper; and, if for delivery outside the Province, a permit from the Province in which the shipment originates. *Note: A permit is not required when such a package originates in P.E.I.*

Dead birds or their parts, nests or eggs protected under the Migratory Birds Convention Act will be acceptable for shipping during the closed season only if the shipper provides a permit from the Canadian Wildlife Service, Environment Canada, Ottawa ON. K1A 03

Hides, pelts and other articles emitting offensive odors are not acceptable for shipment.

Plants. The Plant Quarantine Act prohibits or restricts the movement within Canada of certain plants, plant parts and soil. Contact Agriculture Canada.

Other Dangerous Goods Please check with your post office whether the following items can be shipped:

Explosives – signal flares, fireworks, ammunition, dynamite, black powder, fuses, toy and starter pistols, detonators.

Flammable Solids – lithium batteries, mothballs, matches, sodium, phosphorous, magnesium, fire starters.

Radioactive Materials – medical isotopes, measuring instruments.

Gases – Aerosol products, butane, propane, carbon dioxide cartridges, cigarette lighters, fire extinguishers, compressed gas, cryogenic liquids, mustard gas.

Oxidizers & Organic Peroxides – adhesives, disinfectants, fiberglass repair kits, hair and textile dyes, nitrates, organic peroxides, oxygen pellets, hydrogen peroxide, oxygen.

Corrosives - acids, drain openers, dyes, formaldehyde, bleach, paint or varnish remover, cleaners.

Flammable Liquids – acetone, camping fuel, after-shave lotions, gasoline, paints, enamels, lacquers, perfumes, solvents, thinners, turpentine, petroleum distillates.

Toxic & Infectious Substances – arsenic, chloroform, disinfectants, drugs, fungicides, hepatitis, HIV, infectious biological products, infectious blood, wood preservatives, photographic chemicals, herbicides, pesticides, insecticides.

Misc. – asbestos, battery powered devices with battery installed, dry ice, hazardous wastes, self-inflating life preservers, air bags, strong magnets, gas-filled shock absorbers.

PRICING AND THE LAW

We've discussed pricing quite extensively throughout my book, however, there are certain aspects of pricing which may lead you to walk the fine line of the law. These cannot be ignored. Common sense marketing will tell you that whenever a customer feels cheated or a competitor feels that you are practicing any form of deceptive advertising, you could land yourself in hot water. When dealing with pricing issues, avoid these like the plague:

- **Bid Rigging:** When negotiating for a job contract, don't disclose information to third parties, keep your bid secretive.
- **Product Dumping:** Don't try to toss large amounts of your product on the market at fake low prices.
- **Predatory & Limit Pricing:** Do not lower your prices so low that you

squeeze competitors out of the market. Or sell so close to cost that you hold competitors at bay.
- **Price Fixing:** Do not discuss your pricing policies with your competitors in any which, way or form.
- **Disguised Price Fixing:** Don't agree to offer the same credit requirements, same down-payments, or sell off your products/services at the same price as competitors.

FULFILLMENT OBLIGATIONS & REFUNDS

As a direct response entrepreneur you will most likely have to deal with mailing or shipping out your products. Make it an engraved rule to always fulfill the same day you receive an order. Even if you are receiving personal checks as payment, go ahead and ship the product out any way. You will have only a handful of bounced checks that will require collecting, and there is no sense in penalizing all your other customers and making them wait for a few bad apples. A good collection agency or lawyer can assist you with the few that you aren't able to collect.

The Federal Trade Commission regulates and controls undeliverable or late merchandise when involved with mail order operations. You are legally bound to deliver your product to the customer within 30 days from the day you receive your order. If you promised 45 days (or any other time period) in your advertisements, then you have to deliver by that time. If for some reason you cannot deliver, you have to contact the customer and advise him of this. You have to give the customer a choice of either canceling his order and getting a full refund, or waiting for his delayed product. Any notices have to be in writing and sent by first class mail. If you run out of inventory and have to cancel an order, you have to again let the customer know immediately and send him a refund promptly.

In all fairness to your customers, please offer refunds as quickly as possible and without arguing. Your client's put their trust in your hands when they place an order. You can't please everybody every single time, so you will undoubtedly get returns on your products. When this happens, the policy "the customer is always right" should hold true.

You might decide to hire a "fulfillment company" to take your orders, package your product, and ship directly to your customers. I have found that by keeping the fulfillment duties "in-house" I can better monitor the quality of my operation, and make changes quickly if a problem becomes evident. I admit, I am a bit of a perfectionist, which is why I have taken the "in-house" route. You may find that using a "fulfillment company" will service your needs better.

THE LOWDOWN ON EMPLOYEES

As your business grows and matures into a solid and profitable venture, you will undoubtedly require the assistance of employees, for the simple fact that your underlying goal will be to work less and make more money! You will have to deal with the employee situation as some point. In the direct response business, many of the core activities can, and should, be farmed out. Tasks like: folding flyers, envelope stuffing, administrative work, accounting, cleaning the office, data entry, can all be accomplished with the help of employees. These tasks bog down the creative entrepreneur. Face it, we are not born managers. We are go-getters. We want to do it all ourselves to make sure it gets done right, and we hate having to delegate.

My words of wisdom on this subject are varied and require some detail. I have run businesses in the past with up to 20 employees operating from large commercial locations, as well as operating lean-and-mean profitable one-man businesses. My main motto for using employees is as follows:

Keep a lean and streamlined business infrastructure, keep as much of your funds out of employee salaries, and use employees ONLY WHEN YOU POSITIVELY KNOW THAT THEIR WORK WILL INCREASE YOUR HOURLY PROFIT POTENTIAL.

Here I will illustrate my employee logic as it relates to my ad agency business. One of the areas of service that we offer to our builder/developer clients is the tracing of architectural house plans. Usually the standard model home is a two-story, so we would have to draw the basement, ground floor and second floor. These are computer drawn plans, which generally take approximately three hours to complete. The price that I charge my clients is usually around $300 for this service. Now if I was to sit there and draw them myself, I would be earning $100 an hour. Not a bad hourly pay, you say? I suppose so…but my plan is to make more money by doing less work. So I phone in one of my student freelancers, who I have personally trained to draw plans such as these. I pay my freelancer $50 per plan (piecework). He completes the house plan. The job is not perfect, and I have to spend half an hour correcting his work. The final outcome though, is that I end up making $250 for 1/2 an hour of work. Meanwhile, the 2.5 hours that I save I am marketing, creating, thinking, and **USING MY BEST TALENTS TO MAKE ME EVEN MORE MONEY!**

It can be said that whenever an employee can offer you:

- freedom from the day-to-day business operations,
- allow you extra time to spend with your family and friends,
- can handle administrative or accounting tasks on their own,
- able to tackle and solve problems on their own so you don't have to,
- and can make you a tidy profit at the same time…

Then go ahead and hire them!

Employees, unfortunately, do come with their own set of disadvantages as well:

- They get complacent and lazy
- They demand raises, pay increases and benefits
- They bring their personal problems into the work place
- The hiring and training process can be long and time-consuming
- Their work has to be double-checked for mistakes
- They are not entrepreneur-minded so you can't expect them to act as you do

Despite their disadvantages, the immense benefits of employees cannot be refuted. So you will definitely use some great tips and tricks from my experiences on how to handle them and manage them. Kindly note that each business is different and will require different management styles. Try to take bits and pieces of my tips and "tweak them" to fit your business needs. So here they are:

• Try to use only freelancers with no set salary range. Use them only when the workload dictates. Pay them piecework rather than an hourly wage, this way you can gage greater control over your expenses.

• Have every employee/freelancer sign a work contract – no exceptions. Clearly spell out the pay structure and an easy exit plan for yourself if the employee does not work out.

- Don't hire a Mini-me…or a miniature version of yourself. Hire the talents, experience and knowledge that you don't already possess.
- When hiring, use simple tests to find out if their skill levels are up to par, or if they match what is written on their resume (some people do lie on their resume).
- Take your time in the hiring process. Ask to see licenses, diplomas and credentials. Check references diligently, call at least three of their previous employers.
- Fire quick. When cutting staff members…use an axe (why drag it out?). It's usually the problem employee that keeps working for you…which causes the most headaches.
- Allow for creative freedom in the home office. Let your employees come to you with their ideas and feedback. Hold brainstorming meetings together.
- Praise them in public—reprimand them in private.
- Create the most comfortable and fun work atmosphere that you can.
- Give employees high expectations and goals and monitor them to see if they are progressing.
- Practice an open-door management style, so you can be available to handle employee concerns and to keep a watchful eye over them. Be a good listener.
- Be respectful, don't yell, shout, or lose self-control. You have to lead by example. Would you want your employee to yell at you? Besides, a predatory management style rarely works.
- Learn to recognize high-flyers early in their career and give them some kind of bonus or extra compensation so that they remain loyal. Consider even a small ownership incentive or a commission from the net sales of the business. You never know when your competitors will be hovering above like vultures, looking to steal your key people out from under you.
- Enforce a zero-tolerance office error system. Check and double-check.
- Learn to sniff out the warning flags when issues arise. Face these problems head on, don't beat around the bush or procrastinate…this will only make matters worse.
- Rotate staff members into different positions regularly. This will keep them fresh and interested in their work. The Japanese use this business strategy with great success.
- Minimize the financial risks by not allowing staff to handle cash orders. Never allow a staff member to have signing or withdrawal authority over your business account.

HOW TO CREATE AN UNLIMITED INCOME SITTING AT HOME IN YOUR PAJAMAS

- Never lose sight of the main categories (see below) of employment positions, and hire staff to fit these categories. Take note of employees with multiple specialties who can be rotated.

Marketing, sales and business-generators! (this is one of the most important)
Data entry, processing orders, and fulfilling orders
Administration positions
Management
Accounting and bookkeeping
Human resources (in larger companies)

WINNING CUSTOMERS FOR LIFE

Without a doubt, keeping and reselling to your existing clientele is a lot easier, it costs considerably less, and uses up far less energy on your part. In fact, studies indicate that it takes six times as much cash finances to market and land a new client than it takes to retain an old one. By the same token, approximately 70% of customers that do decide to go with one of your competitors has made the decision to depart because of poor customer service. Viewing the above statistics, it is easy to see that it makes clear sense to keep the customers that we do have, and try to make them our lifetime customers. How can we accomplish this daunting feat? I offer a brief summary of cutting-edge pointers:

- Start off by creating a professional image in the eyes of your prospects. Many of them will never get to meet you in person, so the only impressions they get will be your: web site, business cards, stationary, letterhead, envelope, and other printed materials. Don't skimp on these items. Use the best paper you can afford, and hire the skills of a graphic designer to assist you with the design. Don't lose dollars by bending down to pick up pennies. Make sure your company name clearly indicates the business that you are in or the products that you sell. In addition, try to keep all the elements of your marketing material to follow some kind of identifiable consistency so that you can build brand awareness. What is considered good, consistent branding? Think of the Nike swoosh!

- Keep in touch with your customers. Use the mail, the fax, e-mail, and the telephone. A strategy actually exists which will help you bring in a large volume of new business. I will reveal it to you: **Send out more promos on a more consistent basis** to your existing client list. So if you usually send a promotional piece once a month, try sending one out every two weeks. After a while, the results of higher revenues will surprise you.

• Send a survey to your customers so that they can indicate areas of weakness or improvement within your new company. Some key points that you should include are:

How are we doing at the present moment?

How can we improve in the future?

As well, create and ask specific questions on: reliability, quality of product, speed of the service, accessibility issues, price, overall value, listening ability, how well do we tailor to the needs of the client. Don't forget to ask about the overall appearance of: the home office, sales material/stationary/image and your customer service personnel. Your final questions should be directed to whether the customer was fully satisfied, and if he/she would give you a referral.

• Put your feet into your customers shoes. Think of what their likes and dislikes are. They will be the lifeblood of your new business, so get to know them as intimately as you can. What are their deep, hidden wants and needs? How can you satisfy those needs?

• Find out where your customers are biting, before you go fishing. It does not matter if you have found the cheapest advertising medium in the world, if your customers are not responding to this medium, then put your advertising dollars somewhere else.

• Reliability is one of the key outcomes a customer will look for when deciding to do business with you. Make sure you respond by:

–servicing all the key points you said you would

–doing it within your proposed budget

–doing it within the deadline you had promised

–doing it with the least amount of energy on the clients part

• Be a master tailor. Tailor your products and services to meet your customer's most desirable wants. Because you are a small company, you are nimble, you can move quickly to offer personal customer service and change your business slightly to satisfy your clients. As you continue to treat your customers in a special, personal way, your competition slowly loses market share.

• A sale without a referral is like a fish without water. After you have made a sale and your customer is 100% satisfied with his purchase, this is the opportune time to ask for a referral. Send out referral certificates that offer a discount or a free gift to your customer base. Ask for referrals whenever you have any successful contact with one of your customers.

• Send your customers thank you notes, birthday cards, anniversary cards (the date the client first made a sale with your company) and Christmas cards. Clip magazine and newspaper articles that relate to your customers and mail it to them with a little note saying: "I thought you might like an extra copy of this to give to your friends and family." Your client will appreciate this act of caring on your part.

• Here is a strategy to catch your clients off guard and build a strong client following: Increase your prices by 5%. After you have received payment from a client, send him a 5% refund check back, along with a discount certificate for future buys with your company. Include a thank you note that says "We appreciate your confidence and continued business." There is a high possibility that he will do business with you again in the near future.

• The 80/20 rule. After doing business for 17 years, I have come to the conclusion that 20% of my customers give me 80% of my business. Therefore, my marketing plan is laser-focused to these "golden" 20% clients. I do twice as many mailings and promos to these clients. You should do the same.

• Become an expert in your field. This is a hot strategy for getting clients to come to you, but also to build credibility and repeat sales. All you have to do to become an expert is basically become a publicity hound:
　–Teach at community colleges or universities (if a relevant course exists)
　–Make appearances, give speeches and free seminars
　–Create a press release and send it out to media outlets (more on this in the next chapter)
　–Become an author and offer free articles in newspapers and magazines
　–Become a freelance author for online publications
　–Publish and send out your own newsletter

• The silent unhappy few. One mysterious, but relevant marketing secret is this: For every one of your customers who complains – there are a large number who WERE THINKING THE SAME THING BUT DID NOT COMPLAIN. The silent customers are the ones that leave you in the cold. So take note of your complaining clients and make the necessary changes to improve your business operations. It will be in your best interest to actually welcome complaints and make it easy for your customers to do so—in the long-run it may even save your business.

• Handling the complaining client is a science all on its own. It is a part of business, so this is how you should handle the unsatisfied client:

1. Listen emphatically, and never interrupt the client until he has finished venting his anger.
2. Show total understanding on your part, and that you will take full responsibility for the problem.
3. Always re-confirm what the client has disclosed to you, and make sure everything is clearly understood.
4. Without blaming, ask the client how he would like the problem resolved.
5. If you can resolve the issue, do so promptly and during that initial phone call. If you cannot solve the problem immediately, tell the client when you will solve it...and then do it.
6. Call the client back to confirm that all has been resolved to his satisfaction. Call again about a week later. This will show the client that you care.
7. Keep a database of all complaints, the issues involved, and the resolution dates. You will see patterns emerging, and this will indicate to you the areas in you company that need a major overhaul.

- When panning for your fortune, seek out the gold nuggets that are near the surface—don't spend your time mining for the deep treasures. Direct response is about volume, and making as much profit from the clients that are readily available. **Spend your time attracting a large volume of smaller clients, who are nearest to you— and who are ready to buy.** Many a businessman has done the time-consuming mating-dance with the large client, only to discover smoke and mirrors—and no pay day in the horizon.

- Enforce and advertise a 101% client satisfaction guarantee. Why 101? Because it is good business practice to give your customers something extra and unexpected. It can be something small, but valuable in your customer's eyes. If your competitors do not offer guarantees, this is an opening for you to advertise yours—and stand out from the crowd! When creating your own product or monitoring your service, you will have greater control over efficiencies and ways of eliminating errors and product deficiencies. Make it known to your customers that you have a 101% guarantee in place by:

  –advertising it in every single medium you can,
  –putting it on all your sales literature and printed material,
  –creating a separate certificate to highlight this unique selling feature.

- Make a lasting impression every time you speak with one of your customers. Think about it this way: After you put down the phone, what impression have you made that will make this client do business with you in the future...rather than with one of your adversaries?

CUSTOMER TESTIMONIALS

There is no better way to build credibility for your business ventures than by using honest and believable testimonials throughout your complete marketing campaigns. I didn't get into the details of testimonials in the last chapter when we were learning about creating irresistible offers, because at that point we were testing our ideas and we didn't have a customer base to draw testimonials from. Now, as you begin to deal with customers and make sales, you will be in the prime position to ask for and get testimonials.

Always know that people are generally followers—not leaders. They are especially fearful of new products and services. You can't really blame them can you? Would you spend $500 for an unknown product or service, without some kind of proof that others have gone before you and benefitted by the sale?

Similarly, it is human nature for people TO NOT GO OUT OF THEIR WAY, or deviate from their set routines. Face it, a client will not send you a testimonial on his or her own, without a little coaxing on your part. That is why it is so important to take an active approach in generating customer testimonials. Here are a few tips on this subject:

• When receiving any glowing thanks or witnessing any exuberant happiness from one of your customers, this is the best time to ask them for a testimonial.

• When shipping out your product, include a postage-paid return envelope as well as a testimonial form for your customer to fill out and mail back.

• Offer a small premium gift, or a discount certificate in return for testimonials. Don't ever offer to pay people cash—this would be dishonest. If it ever leaked out to the public, you would lose face...and business, very quickly!

• You must always get customers to write and sign an approval disclaimer, before you can publish their testimonial in your sales material. Equally as important, have them sign an approval if their testimonial will be used on radio or television advertisements.

• In printed material, try to include the full customer name, as well as the city, province (or state) that they reside in. Printing only initials of names looks a bit unbelievable.

• Always use a recent and clear photo of the customer in your print advertising.

• Many people welcome the opportunity to receive their "15 minutes of fame" by appearing on your literature, radio and TV advertisements. Up-sell this human desire of being famous, by stressing that many customers achieve some form of celebrity appeal because of the media exposure. Because of their hungry egos, your customer's will gladly make their appearance for FREE without asking for any compensation in return.

• This is such a powerful strategy: use celebrities to try your products and give you their testimonials. So how do you go about getting Madonna's telephone number? (joke) Actually, any well-known public personality type can work wonders for generating "buzz" with their testimonial. Sample personality types you can seek out: best-selling authors, radio disc jockeys, TV news broadcasters, doctors, lawyers, company CEO's, athletes and politicians.

WHY YOU SHOULD DO MULTIPLE MAILINGS

When you are creating marketing campaigns in which the client is contacting you to request further information, your goal should be to convert 20% of these leads into paying customers. In other words, if you mail out 100 of your sales letters to interested prospects, you should be convincing 20 of these prospects (eventually) to purchase your product or service. This might seem extremely high to you, as compared with statistics available on the subject. However, statistics don't take into account the strategies that you are learning in this book! So here is another little secret that increases responses:

DO A MULTIPLE MAILING BLITZ TO YOUR MOST INTERESTED LEADS

When you are marking-up your products and services as prescribed earlier, you will have the elbowroom to do extra mailings to convince your leads to buy from you. A thorough marketing strategy would be to do a total of three separate mailings, spaced out about 21 days between one another. Change the copy of your sales letter slightly for each mailing that you do, and test different headlines while you're at it. Make your third and final mailing the most powerful piece, and throw in an extra premium gift or reduce your price approximately 10%...to convince those stubborn fence-sitters to buy!

To complement your multiple mailings, do an e-mail blast and add a telemarketing blitz into the mix. This marketing campaign should last about 42 days. Here is a hypothetical example of how this campaign may play out to produce a nice little income: you place classified ads that generate 100 leads per week (this is an extremely conservative estimate by the way). After one month you will have 400 leads. A 20% conversion rate would be 80 sales. If you were selling a $200 item, you would have grossed $16,000. Even after paying expenses, I'm sure that you can survive quite nicely on the remaining monies!

FORGET ABOUT POST OFFICE BOXES

I used post office boxes a couple of times as my return mailing address. The reason for this was that I was mailing sensitive and personal material in which I didn't want my clients to know my home address. Unfortunately, my prospects saw through this "veil of uncertainty" and placed fewer orders. Trust me, P.O. boxes give an added touch of concealment that is not welcomed. Plus, by using a physical address, you will notice that quite a few of your local clients will want to meet you in person and come to your home office. You will get more orders by using an actual street address.

SHIPPING C.O.D., SHIPPING IN GENERAL & TAXES

This seems to be a gray area when beginners first get into the direct response business. They are perplexed about whether they should or shouldn't ship C.O.D. My experience tells me that it can work, but you have to build the high return rate across the board and raise your prices slightly. When sending out shipments this way, expect 30% of them to be returned unclaimed or refused by the customer. Many people are not at home when the package is delivered or they do not have the payment handy. The disappointing part is that it will cost you $6-$10 depending on the weight and size of the package. In my business, we put an office policy in place where we would time our shipments and phone the client in advance to advise him that his package was on its way and to have his payment ready. This seemed to help—somewhat.

C.O.D.'s are convenient in that the post office does all the collecting for you, and sends you a nice money order for your troubles. You may want to compare using a major courier or your postal service. Here in Canada, I find that Canada Post is very efficient with the quality of their service. Our postal service rarely loses a package, and their collection methods are fantastic. In the United States, I have heard that UPS seems to offer better results when collecting money for C.O.D. shipments. You must compare both services to see which one is more affordable and convenient for your needs.

Canada Post will usually attempt to deliver your package immediately. If the customer is not at home, the package is returned to the closest post office in the area. Your customer will then be mailed a number of reminders, usually one per week, that a package is being held for him. Canada Post holds onto packages for approximately three weeks before returning them to you. It may be wise to send your packages using Express Post. Using this service, Canada Post guarantees delivery within one to three business days. This will be very beneficial, as long shipping times will allow your customers more time to change their minds about picking up your package.

Another great service of Canada Post is that they offer commercial customers cheaper prices, as well as a convenient at-home pick-up service. When your business grows to where you are mailing over 10 pieces a day, I would advise you to open a commercial account. Canada Post will bill you every month for the packages you mail out.

There is no need to insure your packages, as the extra expense is not really worth it. If any of your clients call to complain about a product which was not received, simply send him out another one, no questions asked. Don't worry, you will not get that many lost packages, so it won't make a considerable dent in your wallet. The only time to really insure something is when it is a luxury item, or something priced in the neighborhood of $500 (or more).

Keep an eye on your product's weight, as this will add to your mailing costs, and to your expenses. There are discounts for certain weight classes. Always try to stay just under the allowable maximum so you can pay less. I won't mention any exact prices here, as they are bound to change by the time this book is published. Compare courier companies, and your local postal service, and find out which one is cheaper when weight is an issue. On the same note, stay away from shipping crystal, porcelain, or glass. There are always extra costs involved with these products (like the bubble-wrap material, and the additional weight).

Collecting sales tax is another nightmare all of its own. Here in Ontario, we have two taxes to collect (PST & GST) which total 15%. When asking your clients to figure out the tax themselves and write it on the order form, this usually results in many errors on their part. Many times in the past I got shorted when asking the client to calculate the taxes. Later, I decided to be smart and started including the taxes in my prices. You should do the same. But keep in mind, things get complicated when mailing outside of your originating locality. In Ontario, we are required to pay only the Province's taxes where the main office is doing business. In the U.S., the tax laws vary from state to state, so again I advise you to check in your area.

CREDIT CARD MERCHANT ACCOUNTS

It has become almost indisputable that in order to attain large sales in the direct response business you will have to acquire a merchant account. This in itself can turn out to be a tall order to fill, because a few dishonest mail order operators have raised the warning flag to the companies that offer these accounts. And even the honest folks who have solid return policies can anger the merchant companies with their high numbers of returns. Getting a merchant account can increase your sales by approximately 30%, simply due to the fact that they are so convenient to use, that customers generally prefer to pay in this way.

The major credit cards that can be accepted via a merchant account are: Visa, Mastercard, American Express & Discover. Fees vary from card to card, but can range anywhere from 3-4% of total sales. There are also monthly fees in the neighborhood of $10 – $15 per card. You will need processing computer software to process orders from your computer. Software is available for both Macintosh– and Windows–based computers. You can also process orders over the telephone by using a system called an IVR. The IVR automatically does an authorization and then processes the amount you specify.

As mentioned above, the requirements for getting a merchant account are quite tough. You may be required to be in business operating under a company name for at least two years before you can even be considered. You will be asked to give a deposit of approximately three months (or sometimes more) of your projected revenue. This is to protect the merchant company against fraud and a high number of chargebacks (which are arguments or rejections from potential customers). There are many reasons why a customer may argue over an item on his statement. He may not recognize your company name, he may not have received the product, or he may have received a damaged or completely wrong product. Whatever the case may be, you as the seller will be contacted by the bank so that you can try to resolve the issue with the customer. If it cannot be resolved, the bank will step in and act as the mediator. If you get too many chargebacks, the merchant companies can actually cancel your account. This is definitely not a good thing.

The only advice I can give you concerning merchant accounts it to put it at the top of your priority list and work like mad to get one. If your local banks are too stubborn, look over the internet. Keep searching and don't give up.

HOW TO BOOST RESPONSES THROUGH THE ROOF

Study the following two ads and tell me which one you think will be more successful at generating leads?

Mail order entrepreneur reveals the secrets of how to make $500 per day working from home in your pajamas. Free recorded details. Call today: 1-800-BIG-CASH.

Mail order entrepreneur reveals the secrets of how to make $500 per day working from home in your pajamas. Free, exciting one-hour cassette! Call today: 1-800-BIG-CASH.

If you guessed at the second one, you would be absolutely right! We spoke earlier in my book about the "free bait offer" and how it can raise responses dramatically. Offering audio cassettes are ideal products to give away for free, because of their extremely low costs to duplicate. Not only that, but why hold the prospect's attention for 15 minutes while they read your sales literature....when you can do a full-blown hour-long sales presentation!

When I ran the first ad above, I received some favorable responses. As I continued to test and improve my marketing system, I decided to develop and offer the free cassette in my offer. Would you believe that my responses increased by about 400%? This alone should be proof enough for you to include a free tape in your offerings. Keep a close watch over the use of CD's, as soon they will make audio tapes obsolete. You must be ready to make the shift into CD's when you see the market change.

Along the same lines, if you are selling a complicated product that requires a detailed demonstration, then adding a video with your initial sales package will also generate substantial responses. If you watch infomercials on TV once in a while (and you should watch them frequently if you wish to get into this business), you will notice many companies offering free videos.

A SURPRISING ADDITIONAL SOURCE OF INCOME

As you begin to develop and manage your own database of customers (house list) you will be in a fantastic position to draw additional income from the rental of those contacts. By checking the list brokers in the Standard Rate & Data Service Directory, you will be able to find one in your vicinity. The mailing list broker might ask you for some kind of proof as to how the contacts were compiled, as some doubtful direct response operators compose names through illegal schemes or by taking them straight out of the phone book!

An additional income of $50,000 to $100,000 per year can be achieved, just by renting out your contact names. Of course the more names you have, the more money it is possible to make. A solid starting base would be about 10,000 names. Given, this might not be within your reach until probably a few years down the road, but be aware of this extra income strategy anyhow.

Another key benefit is that in some states in the U.S., the income generated from the renting of contacts is not taxable. If there was any better way to beat the IRS at their own game, then renting out names TAX FREE would definitely rank at the top of the list! You should definitely look into this once you have established a large client base.

THE ELEMENTS OF INVENTORY

The trick when stocking inventory is to have enough to fulfill orders quickly, but not so much as to cause a financial strain on your pocketbook. I only carry an extra inventory of 10 products at all times. Let's say that you have invented a creative product, and have placed a few ads to check the demand your product will have in the marketplace. You get many leads, and you send out your sales material. Sales come storming in at a rate of 50 per week. You have a home-run product on your hands! It is probably safe to contact your supplier and order the material to build 60 products per week.

Besides, the most common delivery time period to advertise is 30 days (or four weeks). Perhaps you have seen in advertisements: "please allow four to six weeks for delivery." The reason mail order operators want such a long time period is that they don't have the product themselves to be able to ship it on the drop of a dime. By giving a 30-day delivery promise, you have three weeks to get the product in, and then one week to ship it to the customer.

The 10-product inventory rule also applies to packaging material. I made the mistake (early in my mail order career) of ordering 1,000 custom-made mailing tubes for a "flop" of a product, and now these tubes are collecting dust in my basement!

The beauty of creating information products is that they can be printed and duplicated within a few days, so stocking large numbers is not necessary. Printing upon demand (or after the orders come in), will allow you to keep your available funds out of bulk inventory—and into more profitable actions— **LIKE DOING MORE MARKETING!**

So, buy the minimum order of inventory, or commit to the smallest amount possible. Follow the 10-product rule. Don't be shy that your suppliers see you ordering petty amounts. And don't worry about paying a little more for the smaller orders, it's a lot better than spending thousands of dollars on unwanted product wasting away in some storage space in your home!

MANAGING THE HOME OFFICE

The following tips and advice will help you in setting up your home office and making sure that it runs smoothly.

Zoning. If you own a split-zoned residence (commercial/residential) you will be in a prime position to open your home–based business, without worrying about zoning issues. For those of you not so lucky, I would again have to tell you to check with your areas laws. I think you can get away with it at the beginning when you are just one person, operating from your kitchen table. As your business grows and you need the assistance of employees, the zoning issue will become a major issue.

Licenses. Most businesses have to be registered, and some need specialized licenses. Make sure you look into this critical step.

Legal Issues. As you run your business operation, you will undoubtedly at some point require the assistance of a competent lawyer to assist you. Finding a lawyer in advance is a smart move. You may want to use a "prepaid legal service," which charges a small fee (about $25/month) and handles many issues for you like: contract review, phone consultations, writing legal letters, collections, small claims court advice, and the writing of wills.

HOW TO CREATE AN UNLIMITED INCOME
SITTING AT HOME IN YOUR PAJAMAS

Insurance. If you start some sort of a service business, you will probably require commercial insurance because your employees will be going into customer's homes. Any accidents/mistakes by your employees, will end up being your responsibility. As well, if you have many delivery people coming to your home, you will want to insure yourself against slip/fall accidents.

Computer/scanner. When shopping for a computer, try to purchase the model which will best suit your needs. This may be hard to accomplish, since new models come out every few months it seems. It may be best to wait a short while to pick up the better model. If you will be creating your own brochures and other advertising material, it will make sense to purchase graphic design software like Illustrator, Corel Draw, or Photoshop. Other software which will be vital to your business may include: list management or database management, accounting and word processing. A scanner for scanning in photos and illustrations may also be useful. Opt for a scanner that can handle legal-sized paper, rather than only letter-sized.

Phones. Try to get a phone with a minimum of two lines, but better yet, one with three lines will probably suit you better. In this business, we get a lot of calls, so you have to be prepared to handle the volume without missing any important leads. Head-set phones are a neat way for your staff to talk for long periods at a time without getting a sore neck. I highly recommend them.

Faxes. Many of the faxed papers that you receive will be for customer and payment information, which will probably need to be filed for back-up purposes. This is why it is best to purchase a plain-paper fax machine rather than a thermal fax machine. Over time, thermal paper fades into obscurity, therefore making it obsolete for permanent record keeping purposes.

Office Furniture. The advice I give you here is purchase the best quality you can, and wear them out, before replacing them. Chairs especially have to be purchased with extreme care. Since you will be spending long hours sitting at your home office getting your new ideas off the ground, only the most comfortable, high-performance chair will suffice. Again, go for quality when shopping for desks, bookcases, filing cabinets, and storage cabinets

More Home Office Tips:

• Make sure to schedule breaks and personal time into your daily agenda. Don't forget to take yearly vacations.

• Create a regular work routine, but be flexible in modifying it if needed. Make sure to be able to work around your client's hours, NOT YOURS.

• Don't do chores in the middle of your work-day (or as we mentioned earlier, delegate the chores to others).

• Try to be conveniently located near your suppliers, the post office and your employees, as this will make it easier to conduct your business.

COLLECTION ADVICE

There is nothing more damaging to your business than doing work or providing a product and then having to wait 90 days (or longer) to get paid. The only other worse scenario is not getting paid at all. Obviously, your receivables are the main artery of your entire business enterprise. If funds don't come in on time you can find yourself in deep financial trouble. Take my many years of business experience and use them to your advantage by studying and applying the following collection advice:

• Whether you are sending out a product and waiting for installment payments, or providing a service, try to do business only with clients who have advanced you a deposit. Depending on the type of business (some sectors are extremely price sensitive) you are in, I would say a 1/3 deposit is an average amount to try and establish. However, you may find that in certain instances you may not be able to charge a deposit because you must remain competitive with your adversaries.

• For operating a service business geared to individuals, I would always ask for references and have them checked carefully. In business–to–business sales, the addition of a credit form should also be standard practice.

• If you start a business which must invoice its services, make it a concrete rule to invoice the day the service is completed. Use e-mail or fax to get the invoice into the client's hands quicker.

• Have an imaginary maximum credit amount for each individual client, and do not give further credit if a client has any past due invoices already (basically stop doing business with them until they pay you all their outstanding bills).

• Call your clients one week prior to each installment due date (or invoice due date) to remind them of the upcoming commitment.

*HOW TO CREATE AN UNLIMITED INCOME
SITTING AT HOME IN YOUR PAJAMAS*

- Begin a firm collection procedure immediately after the 30-day grace period has expired. You can start with simple phone calls and then move into written warnings later on.
- Don't become a wimp if a client is ignoring/hiding from all your contact attempts, keeps giving irrelevant excuses, cannot afford to pay up, or for whatever reason does not want to pay up. If you find out a client is a slow/non–payer, you have to show the prospect your strong side. There is no reason in the world that you should play "Mr. Good-Guy" to a client who refuses to hand you over the funds that duly belong to you. It is definitely time to play hardball!
- If after 90 days you still have not gotten paid, turn the account over to your attorney, a prepaid legal service, or to a collection agency. This will prove to the prospect that you mean business.
- Your final alternative will be to take the matter to court. Do so only if the outstanding amount overshadows the time needed for you to prepare, file and present your case. For example: if your hourly value as an entrepreneur is $100, you wouldn't want to sue someone for $300, as you will probably spend eight hours preparing your case and attending court.

Chapter 5
Propelling Your Growth with Additional Marketing Mediums

You have now thought of a revolutionary idea and have tested it within your demographic market. You are managing your new business and it is showing a nice little profit for all your efforts. Therefore, it is time to dig deeper into the advertising mediums that will further entrench your knowledge and prepare you for the expansion strategies coming up in the following chapter. Most of these mediums are not appropriate for the testing or management phases of direct response. Some of them require deep pockets and large budgets to get them started. As well, a few of them are more suited to relationship building, branding and re-ordering potential, rather than initial testing. Some methods are downright unique and unconventional in nature. So, are you ready? Okay then, let's proceed...

NEWSLETTERS

One of the best ways to keep in touch with your existing client base is to create and send out a monthly newsletter. If you design it yourself and distribute it via e-mail, it can be an extremely low cost method of branding yourself as an expert in your field. Let me disclose some industry tips that will help you start your own newsletter and turn it into a successful venture.

HOW TO CREATE AN UNLIMITED INCOME
SITTING AT HOME IN YOUR PAJAMAS

- Note the different methods of distribution available: handing them out, by regular mail, by fax, and by e-mail. Mail I think, is the best method of delivery. Make sure to include your newsletter in all your outgoing mail, product orders, and other print materials. Faxing is a cheap distribution method, but this should be your last resort because of the poor quality in the finished product. Creating an in-house list of contacts and then e-mailing them your newsletter is a great way of eliminating mailing and printing costs entirely.
- Decide who you will send your newsletter to before you create it. Some people on your list (not limited to your present customers) may be: your employees, suppliers, media sources, industry associations related to your business. You may also want to hand it out at public places where people gather or meet. This way you can get your ideas and messages out to a larger market.
- Market your newsletter on your web site and try to get as many people to sign up for it. Hold contests, offer price discounts, draws, promotions to get people to try your online newsletter. Tell people what the value of your newsletter's yearly subscription is, and then give it away for free to the first number of prospects that sign up.
- If you are not "design savvy," then hire a professional designer to assist you with the design of your newsletter. The same goes for the copy. If you are not a good writer, get someone to help you who is.
- The image of your newsletter is extremely important, so make sure to proof read it carefully for spelling and grammar before it is distributed.
- Plan in advance for the creation and printing of your newsletter. You may have to start preparing it three months in advance. With e-mailing, there is no need to print so you will not need as much time. Try to distribute your newsletter quarterly, but monthly is better.
- Reinforce your credibility by including customer testimonials within the body of your newsletter.
- Keep your newsletter short and sweet. Only one page in length should be fine, at the most two pages.
- Number one priority, your newsletter should be "newsworthy." It should entertain, inform and offer valuable information to your subscribers. Make it personal. Make your opinions be known, but stay away from "racy issues" like politics and religion. Keep it brief and to the point, readers do not have time to read lengthy letters.
- Sell, sell, sell, in a quiet, non-aggressive manner. Sprinkle subtle messages of your services within your writing, and how using your services will benefit

your prospects. Add a call to action at the end of your newsletter. Don't forget to always include all your contact information.

• Research your newsletter ahead of time to find present ideas and news-stories. Old news is exactly that...old. Be fresh and creative with your information. Talk about upcoming events or future promotions. Discuss related industry news concerning your business.

• Sell advertising space within your newsletter. Contact businesses with similar interests to yours and ask them if they would like to place a small ad in your newsletter. Get many ads, and you can offset your design and printing costs. Keep this advertising strategy to a minimum, as one of the benefits of your newsletter is that there is no competition fighting for your prospect's attention.

• Try to add some enjoyable themes within your newsletter to breakup the boredom. Put in things like: quizzes, puzzles, word games, contests, prizes, tips and advice columns.

• Don't forget to charge for your newsletter! Prices usually start from approximately $30/year and can go as high as $200/year for more specialized, niche market newsletters. The income you generate will flow continuously and may even turn into a highly successful profit center all on its own.

PRESS RELEASES

The press release is a fantastic tool to build PR (public relations) on your company and your products, get free publicity and bring in more sales. It is spearheaded directly at the decision-makers at TV stations, radio stations, newspapers, and magazines. The one problem with press releases, is that they are so easy to write and distribute, that the editors of the media are deluged with them on a daily basis. Competition from other press releases is staggering. Your release has to catch the editors attention by being accurate and current, having an attention-grabbing headline, detailing newsworthy facts, and telling a bit about your company and the success you have achieved. Let's review some of the vital aspects of creating and sending out a press release.

• Make sure to do some research on the media outlets you are going to contact before sending your news release out. Your release has to be relevant and highly beneficial to that medium's listeners, viewers or readers. If you skip this all-important step, you will be dead in the water before you even begin your press release campaign.

HOW TO CREATE AN UNLIMITED INCOME
SITTING AT HOME IN YOUR PAJAMAS

• You can get a listing of all the editors in your country by doing a search in the GALES DIRECTORY in your public library. You should double-check the correctness of the information by calling ahead to make sure that the person listed in the directory is actually the right decision-maker.

• Use a cover letter for your news release. The cover letter should be dated, short, and should quickly explain how the following material will be of great interest to the medium's audience.

• Your contact information should be shown at the top (if you are using your company letterhead) as well as at the end of the press release. Make sure the contact information is accurate, so as the media personnel will be able to reach you for an interview or to ask you further questions.

• Always double-space your news release to make it easier for the editors to read. Use margins around your press release. Try to keep between one to three pages in length. Stay away from using colors. Black text on white paper will work fine. When mailing, your envelope should be the standard type with no teaser copy, or windows.

• There is a certain format to follow for press releases. They are always flush left. The first item that should be typed is: **PRESS RELEASE:** Then list the current date in regular (not bold) writing. On the right hand side write: FOR FURTHER INFORMATION: and list your name and contact information (if you did not type the release on your letterhead). Skip a couple of spaces, then in the left hand margin type: **FOR IMMEDIATE RELEASE**. Skip some more spaces and then in the center of the release type in bold capital letters, your headline. Following the headline, will be your factual copy that will back-up the headline.

• I cannot stress how important it is to check the spelling and grammar of your press release. If the editor notices even a few minor mistakes, your release will find its way into their trash can. Use the spell check feature on your computer, and have others proofread it before it is sent out.

• The body copy of your release should be written in the same style as you did when writing your sales letters. Give all pertinent facts and news about your product or service. Include photos, illustrations, and testimonials to further add credibility to your release. Answer the five W's and the H: Who, What, Where, When, Why and How.

• Near the end of your news release, include a company story paragraph outlining facts about your business, your employees, awards, milestones and other achievements.

• Editors and publicists prefer to receive the news release via mail or fax.

More and more of them are however, getting into the technology band-wagon and accepting them via e-mail as well. If you do a search on the internet for editors in your area, and find that they list their e-mail addresses in the contact information, then I would say that it is a good bet to send your press release electronically. Besides, publicists are always on the tightest time constraints, so e-mail is an efficient and quick way to reach them with your timely news information.

• Time your news release so that it arrives at least a week before the deadline date of a publication. If your release is directed to a newspaper, try to get it into the Sunday (or weekend) publication which is typically the largest and has the most space available.

• Always follow-up with a phone call after your news release has been mailed or sent out. Be prepared to play lots of telephone tag to get through to the right individual. Note that 95% of news releases get thrown out, so expect a lot of rejection with this form of advertising.

THE POWER OF FREE PUBLICITY

I cannot even begin listing the endless ways and examples that you can draw upon to create free publicity for yourself and your ideas. If I did have the space and the time, I would be writing a whole other book on this subject alone. Just know that countless individuals and companies use publicity to get media coverage—and best of all, IT'S FREE! The media attention that you generate has the ability to drive sales of your product and/or services through the roof! I will highlight a few of the important steps you should take when embarking on the free publicity route.

Begin by creating your own media kit. Your kit should include:

1. A folder that holds letter-sized paper inside and has business card slots. This folder can usually be found in most office depot stores.

2. A table of contents page to allow the reader to quickly know what the media kit will include.

3. Your press release.

4. Your company story page. Include info about your mission statement, why your company does what it does, how it benefits society, and what special advantages your clients receive by doing business with you. Include a listing of your employees, and their educational backgrounds, experience, and their contact info.

HOW TO CREATE AN UNLIMITED INCOME
SITTING AT HOME IN YOUR PAJAMAS

5. Client testimonials (make sure to get approval first), photos and visuals, and past media news coverage that you may have received.

Target your media kit to the media outlets that you think will benefit the most from publishing or airing your information. Send them your media kit.

Make an introductory phone call. The next step to take is to call up the media source and try to speak to the person in charge, or the one who will make the final decision. Make sure that you have the right person on the line, before introducing yourself and making your "pitch." Quickly explain the benefits of your story or material to the editor. News people are always looking for stories to assist them when they are bogged down by their overwhelming workloads. They are quite selfish in a way, as they are not really interested in your motives for contacting them. Present the editor with valuable information that is urgent and current. *Try to create a unique "catch" - as in an "angle" that relates to your business that you can subtly slide into the news article.* Be persistent if you cannot reach the right individual, but avoid becoming a bug to the media source.

If your telephone call and conversation is well received by the editor, schedule a personal visit to their office location. During your meeting, you can get into the details of your story ideas and how they will benefit the media outlet's viewers. Notice that media representatives are hungry for all sources of information to ease their work schedules, so if your ideas are truly beneficial, you should be able to secure an appointment.

Above all, you have to be unique and stand out from the crowd. If your business is geared to a mass public audience, you will have a better chance of landing free publicity. Media outlets search out interesting and outgoing personality types to appear on their programs. These guests practically guarantee to increase ratings for the show. So try to be an off-the-wall personality, and this will greatly tip the odds in your favor.

Show pit-bull persistence. Mail your press releases, media kits, and make telephone contacts on an ongoing and scheduled basis. Fear not, you will soon realize the tremendous energy that it takes to create and organize a free public relations campaign. In fact, there are many PR services available that can handle this time-consuming task if you do not have the resources to do it yourself.

1-900 NUMBERS

As you begin to hunt for alternative advertising methods to increase your income, you will invariably learn or hear about the possibilities of 1-900 numbers. Callers that phone these numbers are charged a flat fee or a per-minute fee that appears directly on their phone bill. The callers can speak to a live person or listen to a pre-recorded message. A service bureau will be involved in activating the 1-900 service for you and running it through their computer networks, for a small fee of course. Your phone company or long distance carrier will also be in the picture, also taking a piece of the revenues for themselves.

The content of 1-900 numbers is usually centered around sexual discussions, chat lines, horoscopes, dating companies, psychics, and gambling topics. If you will be marketing a legitimate business with the use of 1-900 numbers, your type of market (50+ crowd for example) may not be interested in receiving information in this manner.

I must add that there are many disadvantages with 1-900 numbers that you must be aware of. The key factor is that the regulations of 1-900 lines are so stringent that in certain cases you will be pulling your hair out by the roots, trying to get started and approved. There are certain steps that you have to strictly adhere to like:

1. Filling out a long application
2. Reading and signing the service provider agreement
3. Getting your type of program approved
4. Submitting a suitable script
5. Recording your script (you can do it yourself or have the service bureau do if for you)
6. Furnishing your recording to the service bureau for approval and to have it integrated into their phone lines. There are also "canned" programs (pre-recorded programs) which are available for purchase, but these are virtually worthless if your business or product is unique in any way.

Once your 1-900 line is operational, you will have to get the word out to your prospective customers so that they can put it to use. Advertising can be a very costly way to attract listeners to your 1-900 line. Many media sources will not even run advertisements that have a 1-900 in the copy. If you do decide to advertise to bring in callers, use classified ads, as they are the most cost efficient. I'm sure you have seen hundreds of these types of ads in the

*HOW TO CREATE AN UNLIMITED INCOME
SITTING AT HOME IN YOUR PAJAMAS*

classifieds of your daily newspaper. Limitations and regulations will state that you must clearly: show the costs of the call (per minute or flat fee) next to the 1-900 number, indicate whether callers must be over the age of 18, not be misleading in any way, and identify whether there are any minimum charges or time limits that the callers will be charged.

Because your largest costs will most likely be advertising, if you eliminate these costs entirely, you are almost guaranteed a sure profit. This is why it is to your advantage to use 1-900 number only on your established customer base. You have already paid to attract your customers and prospects into your personal web, so adding a 1-900 feature will generate income which is just "icing on the cake" for you. You can accomplish this extra income by advertising your 1-900 in all your printed material, like your catalogues, brochures, sales letters, newsletters, stationary, and display ads.

Here are some further tips to assist you:
• It is smart to get a 1-900 number that is easily remembered or relates to your industry, so do this at the onset.
• The first 15 seconds of a program are the most imperative, so strive to highlight your "biggest-gun" benefit within this time limit. You don't want callers to hang up before being enticed and drawn into your program.
• Update and keep your information current, so as to generate repeat callers to your number.
• Once in a while, check that your line is operating properly. There is no better way to waste advertising money, than on a 1-900 line that is not working.
• Be careful of charge-backs (or when customers refuse to pay their phone bill), try to resolve these issues directly with the customer.

MAGAZINE PRINT ADS

When your classified ads are working like a charm, one way to snowball your profits is to start placing larger ads in magazines. Typically these types of ads have a border around them, headline/subhead, visual/graphic and the company logo/slogan. Print ads can range from 1/8 size, to 1/4 page, to 1/2 page, all the way up to full-page ads. You can stick with black and white (the cheapest), 1 or 2 colors, or go up to the most expensive, which are full-color ads.

Magazine ads are an extremely "focused medium." That means that you can usually find a specialty magazine whose readership will be inclined to purchase what you have to offer. On the opposite end of the spectrum are TV commercials, which are a "mass medium." Back to specialty magazines though, you can easily find a magazine for markets such as: hunting, fishing, power boating, arts and crafts, dog lovers, luxury sports cars, etc.—the skies the limit! Do a search on the internet and you will find many publications which will be suitable for your market.

One way to know whether a magazine ad will work for your type of customer is to check and see if any of your competitors are advertising in that specific publication. If you do not have any competitors, call up the magazine and see if there is a heading or classification that you can place your ad under.

Magazine ads can get very expensive, and this is definitely one of their drawbacks. Some full-page, full-color ads can go as high as $30,000 for one month. You are basically paying for the beautiful, full-glossy printing, which is of the highest quality (just compare this to newsprint and you'll see what I mean). Keep in mind that if you place a full-page ad, you won't necessarily get twice as many responses as a 1/2 page ad, it just doesn't work that way. Also, you will not pay twice as much for a full-page ad, as opposed to a 1/2 page (you might pay 35% more). Bigger ads draw more attention though, so if you can afford to go bigger, do so.

Magazines usually require at least one to two months' advance notice when booking ad space. That is why they are not suitable for the testing phase of direct response, because we would have to wait so long until the magazine hits the stands. Also, measuring your results may take months to tally up, as magazines usually have a longer shelf-life. They hang around longer. They get left in waiting rooms. They get pass-along readers—that means many different individuals read the same magazine. Think of a magazine purchased by a family, it gets passed around being read by the father, the mother and the adult kids. The problem with this passing-around though, is that we never know if the second and third reader is really in our target market.

After you place your magazine ad, you will notice that the "drag" factor lasts longer than with newspapers. Orders will keep coming in, sometimes many months after the magazine has been distributed. Furthermore, because of their long lead times, magazines are not good for advertising timely specials or sales—as you may end up missing the date you advertised in the ad.

Magazine ads should be designed with the help of a graphic designer. You are looking for knock-em-dead impact…not pretty looking ads that don't do anything. Use a strong headline, as usual. The visual should be one that shows your product or service being used. The visual is actually very important in the

HOW TO CREATE AN UNLIMITED INCOME
SITTING AT HOME IN YOUR PAJAMAS

print ad, so choose it wisely. Don't forget your call to action and your contact info. Remember this is direct response, we are not building awareness, we want to measure results. You can include a small mail-back coupon in your ad that has a tracking code so you will know where the order came from. Also, ask your media representative to inform you if any other ads have a cut–out form on the page behind where your ad will appear. If this gets cut out, your ad will be destroyed. It makes sense to ask for some sort of position guarantee from the magazine. Try to stick near the fold line, in the upper right hand side of the magazine (this side draws more responses). Do not purchase ad space on the back of the magazine, as magazines are frequently placed in plastic covers in waiting rooms, and this will cover up your ad.

If you find yourself with a hit of a display ad, you may want to hire an ad agency to start duplicating the same ad and placing it in many publications for you. They have the manpower and the connections to place ads quicker than you could ever possibly do it yourself. Sufficient savings can also be seen, as agencies may be able to negotiate discounts of 15 to 30% for you, just by placing the advertisements. Beware of running continuously in one magazine though, until you have correctly tallied your results for one issue, and you are sure that the ad is a success.

Magazines usually like to play hard ball when it comes to negotiating discounts for their ad space. Smaller magazines are usually more negotiable that larger, national ones. You may want to have an ad already prepared, and then phone a number of publications and advise them to call you in the event of a last-minute discount. One other trick I heard of is sending 20 different magazines a check at a 60% discount off their regular rate card, and telling them to hold the check and place the ad when they have a cancellation. If it is near a deadline, and another prospect pulls their ad, you may get yours inserted at the discounted price. Supposedly, this tactic will get two of your 20 checks cashed!

RADIO ADVERTISING

Advertising on the radio can be the most cost effective way to reach a very large audience. One reason I believe, is that it is an unappreciated medium. It is not commonly used. Furthermore, radio advertising is a lot cheaper than TV advertising, but surprisingly, it is even cheaper than print advertising too. And radio reaches the biggest market of the population, even more than television!

So don't neglect radio as a viable advertising source.

Since there are many topics to cover when advertising on the radio, I will list them in bullet form.

- Radio listeners tend to be extremely loyal, so when you find an audience that works for you, do a repeat program with that station. Make sure to research the audience of the station before you place your first ads. A great way to decide which radio station to advertise in, is to survey your customers and ask them which stations they listen to on a frequent basis.
- Talk radio stations generally pull better responses than music-based stations. Stay away from the stations that advertise: "commercial free for one hour" or similar boasts of long music playing times. These stations make the listeners very happy, but not us, the paying customers.
- Go for longer commercials like two minutes, rather than 30 second commercials. This way you will have more time to describe your offering. Mention your company name and contact number many times throughout the commercial. Pick a phone number that is easily remembered, like if you are in the car business it might be 1-800-888-AUTO.
- Radio ads are not good for selling a product or service, they are simply good for generating leads, building awareness, and branding. Do your best to get prospects to call, so that you or your staff can convert them into paying customers.
- Use words, and sound effects to create a visual image in the minds of the listeners. Paint a picture, with the use of a unique, memorable voice or descriptive words. Remember, you will not have the power of pictures working for you in radio ads. Make sure sound effects relate to your story, and are easily recognized.
- If you mention pricing in your ad, use an even number like: $30 rather than $29.95 which is harder to say.
- Radio rates are extremely negotiable. If you are advertising as a direct response guru, ask for some sort of "guaranteed results." Stations will know that you can track your ads easily and measure their performance, so they will negotiate. Sometimes stations have 20 different prices for 20 different clients, that is how dramatic their price differences can be. Ask to have a ROS (run of schedule) which means they block off a period of time and book you to run in that block of time during different times each day. Always negotiate to be the first ad in the commercial break, as listeners seem to remember these ads better.

HOW TO CREATE AN UNLIMITED INCOME SITTING AT HOME IN YOUR PAJAMAS

- Try to negotiate a "per-inquiry" payment structure, rather than a flat price per airing. This way you can calculate how many inquiries you will need to have a successful ad campaign and then you can negotiate the price that best suits your budget. Many radio stations will not agree to this payment structure, but it does not hurt to try.
- Since radio advertising is so cheap, use it to reinforce your other marketing activities, for example if you have an ad also appearing in the Sunday paper you can say, "Look in this weekends newspaper on page 3 for our discounts."
- From what I have read and experienced on this subject of radio advertising, better responses can be attained if you read the script yourself and add that "personal" touch. Sure, radio stations do offer to produce the radio spot themselves if you commit to a longer schedule, but results indicate that an announcer/host reading your ad will not be as effective.
- The time of the day that you advertise will have a big effect on the price you will pay. Stations usually break up the day with day-parts. The morning and afternoon rush hours are the most expensive times to advertise in. Middle of the day times (10 a.m. – 3 p.m.) are usually when the work crowd is tuning in, and this audience is very minimal. The evening and midnight shift have the least number of listeners, although they tend to be the most loyal. Radio sales reps usually group late-night spots in with daily programming to sweeten the deal.

TELEVISION ADVERTISING

The television is a force that must be reckoned with. Why do I say this? Because it is the most powerful, the most expensive, and the most complicated of all the advertising mediums available to the direct response guru. Production expenses to put together a commercial can be sky-high. It is also very difficult to buy TV time due to the complexities involved. Which channel do you advertise on, which time slot, and what time of the year? These are all questions which must be answered correctly...the first time. You do not have the funds to correct mistakes when you advertise on television, at least not you, the little guy. Television is definitely not for the beginner or weak at heart! Read the information that I have included here, but know that you will probably not put it to use until you have become a true expert in direct response, probably five to ten years down the road!

Many years back, the grip of the three largest US networks (CBS, NBC and ABC) had a strangle-hold on the market and it was almost impossible to afford to advertise on TV. With the growth of cable television and hundreds of specialty channels, the possibilities are widening and the costs are dropping. It still doesn't make television a cheap medium. Competition is growing on a yearly basis, which is bad for the big networks, but beneficial for direct response advertisers. There are more opportunities of specialty channels to tailor your message to fit the right audience. The broadcast stations audience is a more "mass," broad range market. If your product/service is geared towards a specialty audience, then choose a cable channel and avoid the broadcast stations.

One other tidbit of information before we get into some of the major details of television advertising. Did you know that the average North American watches over 30 hours of television every week? This is mind-boggling in itself, when you compare it to the average work-day. People spend nearly as much time watching the dumb-box as they do working at their full-time jobs! This statement alone should crystallize the power and the reach that television has over our lives. Okay, let's discuss some of the pointers of television:

• When other advertisers pull out of certain spots, TV stations become flexible in trying to fill up the available time. Usually they give the time spot to the highest paying candidate. It may be to your advantage to deal with a media-buying partner who has many years of experience negotiating with TV stations. Ad agencies or media brokers can work within your set parameters and try to get you the best deal possible. Search in the Yellow Pages or on the internet for "advertising agencies."

• Television is an emotional medium. To make your ads effective you have to pull at your audiences "heart-strings" with deep emotion. This is accomplished by focusing your message around one of the basic human desires: love/sexuality, finances, attractiveness, power, respectability, etc. Similarly, your ad has to deliver the message while connoting "warmth" which triggers emotions in the viewer.

• Television is a demonstrating medium, so you want to do a lot of "SHOWING," not telling. The opposite is true with radio advertising where you are "telling." Stick to the longer time spots like 120-seconds, where you will have plenty of time to SHOW YOUR STORY. 120-second spots pull in twice as many responses as 60-second spots (but ironically it is not double the cost – probably only 50% more expensive). A 60-second spot will pull twice as many orders as a 30-second spot. You should avoid the 30-second spots, as you will be rushed to describe your story and you may come across as being

HOW TO CREATE AN UNLIMITED INCOME
SITTING AT HOME IN YOUR PAJAMAS

a "talking-head!"

• The style of your television ad is very important. Try to produce it around a specific "theme": a celebrity spokesman theme, a humorous theme or a children theme. These are the most effective types of commercials.

• For researching your demographic audience, do a search on the internet for these companies/directories:

Nielsen Television Index
Arbitron
SRDS TV & Cable Source

• As with most other advertising mediums, you have only a few seconds to "grab your audience by the eyeballs" and draw them into your commercial, keep them there with the fantastic benefits of your offer, and then get them to take action: like calling your toll-free number to order! Move fast, and get to the point, avoid "fluff," you simply do not have time for it. List the benefits of your offer, use creative visual effects, interesting camera angles and movements, to grab the viewers' attention and lead them through the entire commercial to the final call-to-action.

• The time of the year that you advertise in (because of supply and demand) will have a consequence over the costs of the commercial spot. January through March is the slowest time in television, so you will get the best prices at that time. April through June things pick up and so do the prices. July through September is another slow period, as people are away on vacations or involved with outdoor activities and not watching as much TV. October through November, the pace picks up again with stores gearing up for the upcoming holiday shopping season.

• Time spots are divided very similarly to radio spots, and these different time slots will have different costs. They range from: early morning drive, midday, prime time (the busiest and most expensive time, 7 to 11 p.m.) and late night (which includes the graveyard shift). Instead of producing a 120-second commercial, you may want to try a 30-minute infomercial, time-slotted at a late night audience. Just turn on your television between the hours of 1 a.m. to 5 a.m. and you will see hundreds of direct response advertisers making their sales pitch. Why not follow their lead?

• Repetition is key with television advertising. It will take many commercials for your audience to first take notice, even more commercials to get them to remember it, and further more to get them to order. Quickly…can you remember 5 commercials that you saw last night? It is a difficult task to get your audience to remember your commercial, but repetition definitely helps to cement your offering in your viewers' minds.

• Due to the limited time available, make sure to have your toll-free contact number viewable at the bottom of the screen throughout the whole commercial, so that the viewers will have plenty of time to write it down.

PER INQUIRY ADVERTISING (NO-MONEY-DOWN ADVERTISING)

An interesting negotiating strategy to try and incorporate when hunting for advertising mediums is "Per Inquiry Advertising." This type of advertising is the most risk-free type of arrangement that you can make with a media source because you are in essence not putting any money up front when you book the ad space. Per inquiry advertising can be negotiated in practically any advertising medium (TV, radio, magazine, catalogs, direct mail, newspaper). Your most important goal is to stubbornly negotiate this payment structure every time you or your media-buying partner makes contact with an advertising outlet. With a "Per Inquiry" payment structure, you basically pay the media source a fee out of either every inquiry, or every sale the source generates for you. Usually, the media source will want a cut from your gross sales, and the fees are around 30%. Believe it or not, television is very receptive to "Per Inquiry" payment structures. The reason for this is that if they don't have a commercial to fill in an empty spot, they have to advertise their own programming, which does not generate any income for them whatsoever. The TV stations will most definitely require you to set up your commercial with one of their 1-800 numbers and one of their service bureaus so that they can track your orders.

Radio is a media source which is not very keen to accepting per inquiry advertising, but they may do it on occasion. Radio is unique to television because if they have free spots available, all they have to do is re-format their schedule and add more talk or more music to fill in the gaps. They are not as "hungry" as television is to fill in those empty spaces.

Print is another category that you can use the "Per Inquiry" payment method. If you can find a business that puts out a catalog with similar products to yours, you can arrange for your products to appear in their catalog for a share of your orders. Of course that business will want the orders somehow going through their ordering process so that they can track your sales. You will eventually be required to fulfill the orders to the customers. You can actually ship your products to the company, and they can in turn drop-ship to the customer.

*HOW TO CREATE AN UNLIMITED INCOME
SITTING AT HOME IN YOUR PAJAMAS*

Tracking is key with the per inquiry method. It must be deadly accurate, so that you can calculate whether to keep advertising in this fashion, or revert to the up-front payment method. Make a mental note that you will never be given the best advertising spots with "Per Inquiry," as advertisers consider it as extra income to fill in empty gaps.

REMNANT ADVERTISING (FREE & LOW COST ADVERTISING)

Listen carefully: you may have the most outstanding product on the market today, but if you overpay for your advertising you will fail miserably! As we have already mentioned, your advertising will take up about 50% of your total budget every month. If you can lower this amount down to 40, 30, and even 10%, then it is quite possible that you will make a killing in direct response.

That is why you should make it a priority to get the lowest-cost but most effective advertising each and every time you book ad space!

Advertising space is one commodity that when it is gone...it's gone. Television, radio, and print media sources know this, and since you know it now, you will have a superb advantage over other media buyers. You will be able to negotiate "remnant" or "left over" advertising space to your benefit. When you purchase TV or radio spots, ask the sales rep to throw in remnant space for free. They may ask you to pay a fraction of the cost (a great deal would be 10% off their regular rate card). You should always be happy to receive discounts such as these, but you will not get them unless you ask for them!

Even magazines and newspapers have "soft" periods where they will look favorably to giving you remnant space. One trick is to ask for smaller remnant ads throughout the same issue of the print source, directing readers to your larger ad that you have paid for. Once you have become a repeat purchaser of ad space, the sales reps will get to know you, and that is the precise moment to "hit them over the head" with the remnant negotiating tactic!

With remnant advertising, you must have ads already prepared to the various sizes available, and you must move fast to negotiate and book your remnant ads. Most remnant spots will be last-minute deadline-crunches, so you will have to be ready to make a decision quickly.

THE LUCRATIVE WORLD OF MEDIA OPTIONS

An unknown strategy exists where you can control a large amount of media space or time, for a fragment of the total cost. Similar to purchasing an option on a piece of real estate, it is possible to secure media space for little or no down payment, and then flip it for an immediate profit. Let's look into this by following an example.

Let's say that a radio station reveals to you (after you inquire about the availability) that they have five unused blocks of commercial time available on a daily basis (35 per week). The normal price of each block goes for $500, but since the station is in a bind and not selling the time for whatever reason, they are willing to sell you that time for $100 per block. You pay for one block of time and request an option for the remainder. You may pay for the remainder at a later date, however, you have an option to hold that space and sell it to another buyer. The radio station will probably demand that you sign an agreement stipulating that you will not solicit business to their present customers.

Since you will be heavily advertising, you will have made many contacts and associates in the direct response industry. With a little bit of salesmanship on your part, you can turn around and offer that space that you control for $250 per block of time. Your profit for one block will amount to $150. Since you held an option for 35 blocks, you ended up with a net profit of $5,250 ($150 x 35 blocks of time). It will be in your best interests to ask for a signed document from the media source, stating that you are actually holding an option, and are in a position to sell it. This will make your offering credible, when approaching potential buyers.

Now imagine taking this technique and multiplying it to every media source that you can think of: television stations, magazines, newspapers, etc. I have heard of stories where people have turned this media options strategy into a full-time and highly lucrative venture. If you are a natural salesman and deal-maker, then this may be an avenue that you should consider. Hiring and training staff and then letting them loose to purchase and resell advertising space is another alternative. Every party wins in this situation. The media outlet sells space it could not sell with other traditional means, the buyers you sell to get an excellent discounted price, and you make a truckload of cash in the interim! Good luck in your media options business!

*HOW TO CREATE AN UNLIMITED INCOME
SITTING AT HOME IN YOUR PAJAMAS*

SIGNS AND BILLBOARDS

This is an area of marketing that tends to get forgotten by most direct response business owners. However, the facts are that signs are another method that you can use to direct customers to your business and increase sales. Signs have to do two things well in order to be effective:
1. They have to grab the attention of the viewer (usually with a big headline or a catchy visual.
2. They have to relay the pertinent contact information to make the viewer take action.

If a sign does not accomplish these two items, then your invested dollars will have been a waste.

The problem with signs is that viewers have only a split second to notice and read your message. Billboards are usually placed facing freeways, where drivers are moving at over 100 kilometers an hour. Chances are extremely slim that drivers will stop and write down your contact information. Usually, hotels and restaurants do well when they advertise off of freeways, and direct customers to their establishments. I commonly advise all of my real estate builder and developer clients to include some sort of signage campaign into their marketing budget. We find that a large number of walk-in traffic is generated this way, and the sign programs end up being a hit with my clients!

If you do decide to add signs to your advertising mix, here are some pointers to keep you on the right track:

• Signs are highly regulated in every community, so check with your cities' zoning department about restrictions on locations and sizes. Do not start designing your sign until you have taken this all-important step.

• Signs are a very crowded advertising medium (take a look at a downtown block and this will be proof enough) so do your best to get MORE CREATIVE AND ALSO SPEND MORE MONEY than your competitors. Use an experienced sign graphic designer to assist you with the layout. Use quality materials, as the image that you project will be seen by many passers-by. Get creative with the use of odd or irregular shaped signs and add-ons, inflatable signs (dinosaurs and the like) and 3D signs with various layers.

• Place your sign in slow traffic areas such as inner city streets, where the speed limit is around 40 – 50 kilometers. Cul-de-sacs are ideal. Avoid the highways and freeways.

- The size of the letters you use, is vital for readability and maximum effectiveness of your sign. These letter visibility guidelines should help you. They will tell you how high the lettering has to be in your final sign, in order to be viewable from the various distances.

100 ft. distance = letters must be 4"
250 ft. = 10"
360 ft. (city block) = 16"
500 ft. = 22"
750 ft. = 33"
1,000 ft. = 43"
1,320 ft. (1/4 mile) = 57"

- The phone number is the number one major piece of information and must be prominent on your sign. Make sure that it is large and readable. The phone number can direct callers to your "free recorded message" or to your inbound call center where staff members can lead them through the sales process.

- Get creative with the various materials that are available in the manufacturing process. Some of these are: lighted box signs, neon signs, magnetic signs on vehicles, bag/lawn signs (plastic bags on aluminum legs – suitable for home service companies), metal and steel, hand-painted, 4 color digital output, vinyl, wood, and electronic moving signs.

- Experiment with unusual locations or with the use of props. Here are a few ideas to get you thinking:

1. Place your signs in vacant property lots and/or fields (contact the owners and ask their approval - you may have to pay a small fee for the space rental)
2. Vacant and retail storefronts (get approval)
3. On rooftops of deserted homes or commercial properties (get approval)
4. Paint a sign on the side of an old school bus, motor home, or other vehicle
5. Paint a sign on the side of a building
6. Use A-Frames (two pieces of wood in the shape of an "A" that fold flat when not in use) and move them around to different locations

THE MISUNDERSTOOD WORLD OF PREMIUMS

A premium is a small gift which you give away for free to build your image, create goodwill, and hopefully force your potential customers to call you in the near future. The chief aim of a premium is to project a quality, professional image. These are some old and overused premiums that you may have in your possession, but may not extol a professional image: pens, mugs, calendars, pencils, T-shirts, balloons, hats, coasters and key chains.

When it comes to premiums, take the initiative and vie for the more expensive and valuable-looking one, rather than going for the lowest-priced item. Sure, the numbers may look enticing when you are buying pens at .25 cents a piece, but will they have a strong enough of an impact to enforce a change in your prospects behavior and cause them to take action? I strongly doubt it. Ultimately, you should be looking at premiums that are priced from $10 up to $25 each. The responses you receive from a higher-priced item will be far better than that of a cheap item. Trust me on this one.

Along the same lines, if the **CREATIVE IDEA BEHIND THE PREMIUM** is so bold and unexpected, this alone will cause the prospect to pick up the phone and call you. I once mailed a single dinner roll to 50 of my hottest prospects with a note saying: "I CAN MAKE YOU A LOT OF DOUGH WITH MY MARKETING AND ADVERTISING IDEAS!" Do you know what kind of effect these .50 cent dinner rolls had on my sales after the promotion? They brought me over $50,000 worth of immediate business! Therefore, get **CREATIVE** with your premiums to shock your prospects. If you are in the painting business, send your prospects a paintbrush with a unique slogan or sales letter. If you are in the finance business, send them a one-dollar-bill with the promise to make them more cash in the future. Do you see where I'm headed? Put your thinking cap on and come up with something totally off the wall!

Additionally, a recurring strategy in direct response is to **COMBINE OLD, AND SLOW-MOVING GIFTS WITH YOUR OFFERINGS** (commonly referred to as: "bundling") as an added incentive for quicker orders. Videos, CD's, audio tapes, flashlights, calculators, mouse pads, clocks, wristwatches, pocket knives, miniature models, books/booklets or valuable reports, can all work magically to make an immediate and dramatic impact to your bottom dollar. Make sure to advertise that the premium can be kept by the prospect (as an added incentive for taking the time to order), even if he/she returns your main product offering.

Two final tidbits on premiums—don't forget to imprint your logo and full contact information (including web site address) on them. Service businesses do extremely well with fridge magnets (what a great way to show off your message in your customer's face whenever they open the fridge to eat).

MICHAEL KLISOURIS

JOINT VENTURE AND LICENSING STRATEGIES

Teaming up with other businesses can be a wildly successful income-earning business in itself. One trick is to find businesses that are somehow related to the one you are operating. Make sure that the related business is not in direct competition with your type of business. If you are in the business of deck building for example, you may want to contact landscape contractors. Contact the owners or decision-makers of the related company and strike up a deal to use their existing database of customers to mail your advertising offerings to. Obviously, you will have to arrange for some kind of fee structure to pay the companies for the use of their contacts, but you will have no up-front costs involved in acquiring the leads. This alone can cut your costs considerably and allow you to make a beautiful profit.

Another strategy is to locate mail order businesses with a steady income and whose products you have an interest and knowledge of. If you have a unique advertising formula that you know is certain to bring extra sales to this company, you may want to present it to them as an added income source. Face it…no business has the resources or the ideas to advertise in every single medium available to them.

If they use print ads, they are probably not advertising with radio. If they are advertising in the Yellow Pages, they are probably not using small classified ads, and so on. Similarly, if they are advertising in one local area, they may not have thought of expanding to a different market area. You can try to gain the exclusive rights to market their products/services to another region, state or country in a noncompetitive fashion.

Many times, manufacturers or retailers do not even know how to go about using direct response as an alternate distribution method of their products!

Once you have read and studied my material, the knowledge and expertise that you possess will be extremely valuable!

You can use your knowledge as leverage against these manufacturers/retailers and offer them a proposition that says: "Look what I can do for you, that you may not have thought of!" In essence, you are creating a business by assisting other businesses increase their profits. Offer them a risk-free agreement, where you will create and implement the advertising strategies with your own funds, but both of you will receive compensation in the end. As you gain confidence through experience in the direct response business, you will have almost a sixth sense about what will work and what won't. The odds will tip in your favor. You will confidently create successful joint venture agreements such as these without blinking twice!

A LOW FEE, HIGH COMMISSION CONCEPT

Keep in mind when putting together joint venture marketing arrangements that you don't necessarily have to rape your clients up-front by charging huge hourly fees. It will actually be in your best interests to charge a small fee in creating advertising/marketing campaigns, but negotiating HIGH COMMISSIONS from the resulting sales. This way you can create the campaigns and then sit back and receive an endless supply of residual "kickbacks" from each sale you generated. Actually, large consulting firms practice this concept, as their clients have become wise to the situation of forking out huge amounts of cash on worthless campaigns that don't produce sales. The consultants make the bold statement: If we don't produce results…you don't pay us. Now this takes nerves of steel, however, you can earn substantially 10 times more than a traditional "fee structure" arrangement! You will have your client's best interests at heart and you will make a killing in the process…a perfect win/win situation!

PIGGY-BACK MARKETING

Another creative strategy to incorporate into your business strategies is something called "piggy-back marketing." We touched on it briefly earlier on. This is where a non-competitive businesses advertising material rides along with yours, and goes to the prospects in your database (or vice versa). The other business would split the mailing costs associated with the mailing, therefore creating a cheap advertising medium for both companies. For a small fee, you may even want to personally endorse the other business's products. The credibility and trust that your prospects perceive of you, can be shared with this other company. Make sure that the products/services you are endorsing are of the highest quality, so as not to destroy the good faith that you have already established with your clients.

There are a number of other ways to use "piggy-back marketing":
1. You both can advertise in the same print ad (by drawing a line down the center)

2. You both can advertise on a billboard
3. You can create one printed mailer with both companies on it
4. You can find two other companies and split costs three ways to further reduce costs
5. You can invent another advertising medium where various businesses can gang up together and cut costs

THE INS AND OUTS OF LICENSING

The renting of intellectual property such as logos, images, photos, information, names, slogans, artwork and music is called "licensing." When you create such items and you own them, or you can acquire the distribution/usage rights, then you have the makings of creating a lifetime stream of royalty checks! The truth is, every single person walking on this planet has many million-dollar ideas that flash through their brains. They may not flash all at once, but may trickle in here and there. You have to be ready to grasp an opportunity like this when it presents itself. But how does one go about doing this? The answer is…by building your consciousness through certain actions. Here are the actions that you should undertake:

• **Start thinking creatively to develop your own ideas.** Think like authors, musicians, artists and directors – they work in a frenzied pace to create and then sit back and receive unlimited royalties. Brainstorm with others. Read a wide variety of books, directories, industry journals, magazines and newspapers. Seek out new and unknown settings/music/arts. Deviate from mediocrity. Consult with mentors.

• **Flood your mind with ideas from your public library.** Look at back issues of magazines and see which ads appear over and over again. These are probably successful products/services or they wouldn't be advertising repeatedly. Contact the owners and strike up a licensing deal. Look through patent lists and contact inventors. About 90% of them will not be actively marketing their inventions, and will be eager to hear what you have to propose.

• **Get the "team-spirit" mentality working in your favor.** Stop thinking like a hermit. Start thinking of ways you can partner with existing businesses so that you can both profit. Help enough people get what they want, and in the end you will GET WHAT YOU WANT.

- **Become a master-borrower.** Negotiate and gain control over SOMEONE ELSE'S information, products, inventions, or ideas and build it into a thriving business from the ground up. Go back to Chapter 2 for ways in which to do this.

WORD OF MOUTH ADVERTISING

We all inherently know the effects that good word of mouth advertising can do for a company. Start a fledgling business, provide a notable product or service, and stand back and watch your established customers recommend and bring you new business. It's a wonderful feeling isn't it? The truth is, marketers have to work to establish the right environment for word of mouth advertising to take place. Here are some pointers to get people talking about how great your company is:
- Always do business in an honest and ethical manner. In fact, try to be TOO honest.
- Go overboard with your promotions. When you offer a discount, offer it at 50% not 5%. Give your customers a big incentive to talk about.
- Go above and beyond the call of duty and give your customers something unexpected that they didn't bargain for. A quicker deadline than you promised, a smaller budget than you had originally quoted, a surprise refunded discount?
- Pull at their emotions by getting involved in a worthwhile event that you can tie your product/service with. Hold a charity, support a cause, sponsor an association, help out the less fortunate.

TEEN MARKETING

A huge, wide-open territory of marketing exists today that only a handful of direct-response experts know of and take advantage of. This area, is teen marketing and it is focused primarily at 13 to 19 year olds who love to chitchat. Huge corporations are learning about this marketing weapon, which has an untapped hold on only 1% of the whole U.S. teen population. What is it exactly? It is another facet of word-of-mouth advertising but the teens take it to another level of epic proportions. Listen up. Since teens are the most unrecognized and ignored demographic, they long to be heard, to be cool, to be part of the in-crowd. Offer them products or services suited to them, and they will talk. They will talk via e-mail, chat programs, chat rooms, cell phones, cafeteria gossip, slumber parties, etc. After all, it is "totally cool" to know about stuff, way before others do!

The beauty of it all, is that the teens are not even aware that they are taking a part in helping your company grow. All you have to do is offer them some kind of "inside information, discounts or freebies" and let them do the rest. Use the web as your main marketing method to reach the teens. Web banner ads and e-mail blitzes work wonders. Offer some kind of promotion where the teens have to register by filling out a questionnaire, to win discounted or free prizes. Your main question should be: "how many friends, family members and acquaintances do you speak to on a daily basis?" If they answer approximately 150/day, then those are the candidates that you select to spread the word about your company.

Do not ignore this secret teen marketing weapon, it is truly revolutionary.

THE ROLE OF WOMEN IN ADVERTISING AND IN OUR LIVES

I'm going to let you in on yet another little secret. Sell primarily focused to women! Why? Because they make up a market which is more than 80% of all goods and services purchased. They actually influence 70% of the nearly 100 billion dollar consumer goods market! If you are interested in getting colossal sales, you have to be prepared to change the mind of the woman!

The trends are evident. There are more women in the workforce earning incomes which are slowly matching those of their male counterparts. Family spending has peaked with both spouses earning solid incomes. Women dominate the buying decisions in the family. Realtors know this, that is why they counsel their vendors to spruce up the bathrooms and kitchens of the homes they wish to sell (because baths/kitchens are what sells the woman).

So you want big sales? Focus on the female species. How do you reach them and persuade them?

Try these ideas:

- Show the problem, uncover the solution (use before and after techniques)

*HOW TO CREATE AN UNLIMITED INCOME
SITTING AT HOME IN YOUR PAJAMAS*

boldly advertised as the top headline of your ad. If you offer **FREE NO-OBLIGATION ESTIMATES** and all of your competitor's charge for this service, then make sure that this is your bold advertised headline. The second largest type size after your main benefit should be your contact phone numbers. Make sure the phone numbers are large and bold, but not out of proportion with the rest of the information in your ad.

BARTER ADVERTISING

Get prepared. You are about to learn about the world's fastest growing way of doing business in the marketplace today. This carefully guarded, secret business weapon is called Barter Advertising. Put simply, it is the direct exchange of your product or service for advertising space or other items of value to your business. You can negotiate an exchange for basically anything of value that you need, like perhaps a mailing list of contacts, ad space in a niche magazine, or various business services.

The trick is to realize what your assets are, that another company or media outlet will be willing to barter for.

Your assets can be either tangible or non-tangible. Let's look at both:

Tangible: products or services, real estate, office space, stocks, bonds, options, materials, inventory, cars, yachts, airplanes, employees, database, distribution methods, copyrights, patents, licenses, trademarks, collectibles (art, coins, stamps, gems, gold, jewelry), antiques.

Non-Tangible: your time, ideas, credit worthiness, contacts, reputation, awareness, ideas, concepts, knowledge, training, background, influence, experience, drive, ambition, skills, talents, beliefs, endless drive and energy.

Once you become keenly aware of the valuable assets that you possess, you can move forward and negotiate some kind of barter arrangement that will benefit both parties involved. You can generate more sales and create cash flow without spending a penny! In fact, barter is commonly used by all sizes of businesses with phenomenal success. Small businesses do straight and simple **barter exchanges**. Larger companies use **corporate barter**, where domestic trading of goods or services pass through their accounts-receivables. These deals range from $500,000 and go into the millions. Huge, multinational organizations barter through **counter-trade bartering**. Bartering transactions are valued in the tens of billions each and every year!

Here are additional things you should know about bartering:

• Bartering can be performed via barter networks or trade exchanges. (A trade exchange acts as a go-between the two parties, and also tracks the transaction). You can even look into opening your own trade exchange.
• Other companies are eager to barter with you, because they are probably in a cash-strapped situation themselves.
• Bartering generates new business without any cash outlay, therefore increasing your bottom dollar by huge percentages. You avoid the day-to-day stress of using your own cash.
• You can eliminate many of your monthly fixed business expenses with bartering. Some of these may include: voice mail and answering service, janitorial service, accounting/bookkeeping, equipment rental/lease, security system, coffee service, bottled water, payroll services, lawn maintenance and secretarial services.
• You can use a barter company to get rid of unsold or excess inventory.
• You can become a high-priced middleman, where you introduce companies to one another, put together the barter arrangement, get the contract signed and you earn a sizable commission for your efforts!
• You can barter the services which you do not use on a regular basis. Here are a few: printing (flyers, stationary, etc.), mailing lists, photocopying, copy-writing, graphic design, auto repair, computer repairs, financial planning, signs, travel expenses and accommodations.

The benefits of barter should now be clearly obvious to you. You can earn handsome profits without any money up-front, arrange lucrative middleman deals, and hunt out the endless barter opportunities as companies try to remain competitive in today's crowded marketplace. This tremendous opportunity should definitely not be overlooked. This limitless trading strategy involves too much information for me to try and include it all in my book. I therefore invite you to do a search on the internet to study this business strategy in full detail.

THE CATALOG BUSINESS

If you are the manufacturer or creator of many similar and exclusive products, you can begin to acknowledge another amazing source for distributing your products. This source is through a catalog that you create in-

HOW TO CREATE AN UNLIMITED INCOME
SITTING AT HOME IN YOUR PAJAMAS

house, or by using a catalog company to distribute your products for you. There are many catalog companies that have clever teams of graphic designers, copywriters, and photographers who can take your products and advertise them in their proven marketing catalogs. Many times these companies do not demand any monies up-front, since they need your products probably as much as you need their distribution sources. Usually, catalog companies will want to see some kind of proof that your product is already being successfully sold in other advertising outlets. They don't look highly to brand new and unproven products, as these can be overly risky ventures, especially where large capital is involved in the outset.

For those small business owners who have started to create additional and back-end products, going the in-house route may be a better alternative. Printing a black and white catalog and using staple-binding will most definitely keep the costs down. Probably a black and white version will not be ideal for high end products, but may be sufficient for the products you are going to be selling.

Keep in mind that catalog customers are an extremely loyal bunch and once they order, and they witness how easy and enjoyable the shopping experience is through your company, they will most likely order again in the near future. Here are some basic tips to lead you through the catalog business maze:

• Try an electronic catalog along with the mailed version and see which works best for your products.

• Save and use your catalogs only on your most established, solid clients that have already purchased products from you in the past.

• Sell only the most unique products that you can get your hands on. Products that are not available in stores (or anywhere else) have a better chance of success via catalog sales.

• Illustrate your hottest selling items near the beginning of your catalog, as this is the area most readers will flip through first.

• Do not skimp on photography. Hire the best photographer within your budget to take high quality pictures of your products.

• Always include numerous order forms within your catalogue. Use both loose, as well as attached order forms that the customer must cut out.

• Use as many payment options and payment plans as you can offer.

If you decide to go the in-house route, the quality control benefit that you gain will offset the labor disadvantage involved to: design and distribute the catalog, take the orders, fulfill your products and offer any customer-service related inquiries after the sale. When you deal with a catalog company, they put the money up-front and you simply sell your products to them at a discounted price. They in turn, handle all the fulfillment obligations, and finally sell your product at the marked up retail price. Also note that there are agents and brokers that act as intermediates between you and the catalog companies, and you can contact them in a number of different ways.

Part 3

Chapter 6
Expansion and Advanced Business Strategies

Congratulations! I commend all my readers who have shown persistence and made it this far in my book. We are on the last leg of our journey together, and this final chapter will probably be the most informative and most eye-opening experience yet. In this section, I will present to you the strategies, ideas and advice that you can incorporate into your thriving business, and build it into a booming mini-conglomerate! I wish to mention, that the following ideas vary extensively from one another. I cover a wide area of topics and there is no set pattern in the order that they are presented. I talk throughout my book about exclusivity and creativity and these characteristics cannot thrive with step-by-step systems. They are more a combination of ideas, pieced together to form a unique "success" puzzle as varied and different as every one of my readers is. Success is more of a moving target rather than a stationary one. And I will arm you with all the ammunition you will need to hit your "success bulls-eye!" Hang onto opportunity as we dive head-first into Chapter 6.

THE CONCEPT OF CLONING

One of the methods that wealthy individual's use to multiply their net-worth, is through the concept of progressive **CLONING**. They created one burger joint, and then two, and soon three...until they had thousands of burger joints spread across North America. Our free market enterprise is a wide-open playing field with vast untapped territory. The concept of cloning suggests that: if your idea works well in one surrounding region, you can logically clone it and move it to another region. If your product is successful being marketed via small classified ads, then expand into other regions utilizing the more than 7,000 daily/weekly newspapers that you have at your disposal.

A strategy exists where you move steadily from one region to another "rolling out sequentially" rather than going crazy and introducing your product/service to the whole country at once. Move slowly and cautiously. Start with one region or State, show a profit and then re-invest these profits into more advertising campaigns in other regions. In this fashion, your profits are compounded one on top of the other and your rates of return reach astronomical levels!

INCREASE YOUR INDIVIDUAL WORTH

The money that you earn is directly proportionate to the valuation of yourself and your business through the eyes of your customers. If you produce and sell more products, if you perform more service, your worth as a business will rise. If you assist enough other people to solve their problems or needs, you will surely find financial success yourself. It is all a matter of giving back to society in a large and consistent scale.

So now you're starting to think, "How can I be worth more and make more money?" If you are wondering how to increase your hourly pay from $25/hour, take note that there are individuals earning $20,000 every hour…and some earn even more than that! The main ingredient in increasing your or your company's worth is by acquiring training, experience and specialized knowledge that others do not possess. One way is to study and learn these skills on your own, definitely not the easiest route, but one that you should not abandon. Make it a point to educate yourself in any way that you can. Use books, magazines, courses, seminars and mentors. Of course a quicker way of acquiring the necessary knowledge is to hire it. Our society abounds with unemployed intellectuals looking for the camouflaged security of a paycheck. It ultimately boils down to this: if you can find a way to raise your worth in the shortest amount of time possible, you will in turn rise to new levels of worth yourself!

*HOW TO CREATE AN UNLIMITED INCOME
SITTING AT HOME IN YOUR PAJAMAS*

THE FIVE-YEAR COMPLETE TURNAROUND

One unique characteristic that I have uncovered during my life, and the lives of others, is that a realistic time schedule to attain life-changing goals is five years. If you study the rags to riches stories of various individuals, you will find that many of them have this common pattern. Starting from dead broke or bankrupt, they completely transformed their adversities into super-successes, usually around the five-year mark. I have personally gone from being on welfare and earning $500 per month—to creating businesses that now earn anywhere between $1,000 to $3,000 per day! I went from having no car, nearly penniless, and living in my mom's basement to driving a Mercedes Benz, being in one of the highest income classes in North America, and owning a 3,000–square–foot, five-bedroom house. A number of times, in fact, I have gone through this "roller coaster ride" called life, ultimately turning adversity into success...all in approximately five years.

I share this information with you in the hopes that you will have the motivation to set your own goals and know that they can be reached within a reasonable length of time. As long as your goals are realistic, you can overcome your temporary setbacks, think positively, show perseverance, put your plans into action, and jettison yourself into the ultimate lifestyle that you have envisioned.

HOW TO CREATE A $200,000/YEAR BUSINESS – IN ONLY TWO YEARS

The following is a practical guideline of how I go about creating my own successes, and hopefully by tuning in, you will be able to do the same. I obviously cannot guarantee that you will positively experience the same success, as many unique circumstances have to be blended together to bring about the identical outcome. Use the following information only as a way of stimulating your own creative process. This is how I go about planning and creating a $200,000/year business:

Create an idea filter. Think of an "idea filter" as a huge funnel, that you toss in your ideas on a monthly basis. Begin by deciding on what your passions are. Then create, find, or duplicate business ideas/products that are in alignment with your passions. Next, throw these ideas into your idea filter.

Test your ideas on a continuous monthly basis. Each and every month, test the viability of just one of your ideas, using the strategies I taught you in chapter 3.

You should find a winner in 12 months. As you know, every 10 ideas (and after 10 months) that you test, will probably uncover one winning idea. This one idea will probably produce a minimum of $100,000 year. I have allowed an additional 2 months to err on the conservative side.

Keep your idea filter full at all times. As you test each of your ideas, make sure to create others so as your idea filter remains full. Ideally you will want to have approximately 2 or 3 alternate ideas in your "idea filter backburner" waiting to be tested.

Repeat the above process the following year. Keep the process rolling, keep the idea filter churning, and within two years you should have built a $200,000/year business.

Now imagine what you can accomplish by repeating this system on a repetitive yearly basis. Where do you think you would be five years from now…or 10 years? It is quite invigorating to think that by following this process of systematic progression, one little idea all by itself can produce a nice little "nugget of gold" income. However, a combination of five, 10, or even 15 winning ideas can turn into a virtual "gold mine" of wealth! What are you waiting for…start thinking of your unique ideas now!

USE AUTOMATION PERFECTED BUSINESSES – OR STAY OUT OF THE GAME ENTIRELY

The main thrust of my material has been to enlighten you with a brand new way of thinking. This thinking involves being unique, standing out from the crowd, conceptualizing on your own terms, and creating your own exclusive products or ideas. In the birthing and developing stage of any business, the creator (owner) is trapped by the time requirements needed to bring the idea into fruition. At this point, the creator is the focal point of the organization, and his goal is to mature the company as steadily but as quickly as possible. Once the business is on a sure footing, the owner can turn the reigns over to his staff, or to the unique formulas of the business – and he can sit back and collect the fruits of his labor.

I strongly recommend that you plan your business from the onset and create it with the mindset that it will run automatically at some point down the road.

If it is a business which relies solely on the owner to operate it even one year in the future, then I have no need for it—it is not the right kind of business you should be starting either. If the business requires an owner's expertise, then it is your duty to train well and spread this expertise onto your employees. Do not create a mom-and-pop type business where you are trapped running the business day and night. An automated business brings in residual income or royalties and you make money whether you show up at your home-office or not. You make money while you play golf. You make money while you sleep. Now this is living…don't you agree?

THE VALUE OF CREATING BUSINESS FORMULAS

Business formulas produce anticipated outcomes day in and day out. Formulas can be duplicated and moved to other businesses or cloned into huge empires. It is your goal to create formulas, and build them into your business as soon as possible. With formulas in place you have the insurance that even if you are taken ill or disabled, the business will run on it's own, unharmed in any way. These are the main groupings of formulas that you should be creating and implementing as quickly as you can:

- Marketing and prospecting systems - that bring in leads on their own without your labor
- Sales systems – that sell silently or with the use of trained sales staff
- Management procedures – that run the small day to day duties of the business
- Routine forms, guidelines, policies – that can be duplicated easily
- Accounting systems – which are easily understood, effective & trainable

MICHAEL KLISOURIS

UNREALIZED RICHES

Is it any wonder that the super-rich pay less than 1% of their total wealth in taxes every year? Amazingly, this is very true! Reports from the IRS back this statement with verifiable, undisputed evidence. How do the rich folks get away with paying so little taxes while we have to dish out 30 to 50% of our income at the end of the year? You might think that they use some secretive tax loop that only they know of. Not so. They use an ancient tax law that says that you don't have to pay taxes on unrealized capital gains. It's easy and perfectly uncomplicated to model your own businesses around. Basically, you start a company, build it, watch it grow and put most of the profits that you earn back into the business (or hold onto your shares and don't sell out).

Similarly, you can buy stocks of other companies, or real estate, and hang on for the long term, steadily building a large net worth. Shifting your assets from income producing vehicles to equity producing vehicles is what it's really all about. Other equity vehicles can be: bonds, mutual funds, rental real estate and royalties.

By the same token, the super-rich own shares in corporations, they don't punch a clock and earn a 9-5 income. The incredible tax advantages, accounting, and liability advantages, that being part of a corporation offers cannot be argued. Perhaps the most attractive feature is protection from the lawsuits that are rampant in both Canada and the United States. It reminds me of some ridiculous figure I once read that an American is sued about every five seconds in the U.S.! This alone should be motivation enough to learn all that you can about corporations and the protection that they can offer you. If you have any sizable estate built already, you would be wise to check into it without further delay.

DIVERSIFICATION IS KING

The reality of the future is that it is a complete unknown. The masses in our society move along day by day, in their salaried positions believing that they have long-term security. The fact of the matter is, all they really have are a pair of golden handcuffs. Employers give just enough of a comfortable income to pay your bills and survive. And with two income families that are quite the norm nowadays, employees get by and live paycheck to paycheck. What a boring existence!

HOW TO CREATE AN UNLIMITED INCOME SITTING AT HOME IN YOUR PAJAMAS

When the smoke screen fades, society will be in for a big surprise. With the revolving doors of corporate businesses, and the unpredictable economic climate, one can never really be sure when that one source of income will dry up. That is why you should begin at once creating additional income sources, to bail you out during the bad times. Bad times can be any one of these, or a combination of two or more:

Your product becoming obsolete (how many vinyl records do you own?)

Competitor's nipping at your heels (introduction of discount outlets or super stores)

A surprise shifting of trends or demographics

Seasonal cash lulls

Unexpected illness or disability

A recession

As you create, implement and get your first business on a sure and profitable footing, begin immediately working on your next business idea. This is the very strategy that is incorporated by the wealthiest individuals in North America. Take Donald Trump for instance. Not only is a he a real estate developer, but he is also: a landlord, a published author, owner of a bottled water company, owner of a modeling agency, publisher of a board game, a TV producer, an actor, a casino owner, a hotel owner, and on and on. Mr. Trump understands the value of diversification…he lives it, and breathes it on a daily basis.

Use creativity when building you new businesses. You can build them **laterally** (or one beside the other) where one company relates to one another. One example of this strategy: if you own an exterior painting company, you can start including window washing and gutter cleaning as add-on businesses. Alternatively, you can build **stacked** businesses, where one mother company gives birth to a high stack of similar or unrelated company's. An example of stacked: if you decide to get into the information selling field you can also start the following businesses: graphic design, advertising, marketing, CD duplication, video/audio duplication, printing services, copy writing, and mailing list broker.

Diversification guards against unexpected surprises, personal ignorance, inexperience and incorrect assumptions. Be smart…diversify into multiple businesses as soon as it is feasibly possible!

CREATE A MONOPOLY

Why get in at the bottom of a product or service industry and kill yourself…battling the competition to get a piece of the market? This seems very foolish to me. On the other hand, you can create a revolutionary idea or product and vault yourself into the number one position. Invent a trade secret or ingredient that cannot be reverse-engineered. Invent a completely new business out of thin air. Build a brand new sub-category of an already existing business sector. Do business in a unique and surprising way.

Gain a dominant position and then sell your wares at attractive, but not exorbitant prices. Keeping lower prices (but high profits due to high volume) will not attract the unwanted eyes of the competition from looking your way. This strategy will allow you to quietly become the sole leader…to dominate your market and make a killing!

BE ON THE LOOKOUT FOR HIDDEN OPPORTUNITIES

There is nothing worse I believe, than living your life day by day in a trance, totally unaware of the treasures that surround you. I'm sure you have heard of the famous saying "one man's junk, another man's treasure"? This saying exemplifies the core strategy of being aware of hidden opportunities, and having the courage to act on them, as the masses blindly pass them by.

Stories abound of successful business people who accidentally came across an untapped or under-exploited product or service, grabbed hold of the reigns, and rode the success horse into the horizon! People have built million dollar businesses on junk that others leave at the side of the curb. Others have profited by buying the worst looking real estate (with overgrown grass on the lawn, broken windows, etc.) in the best neighborhoods, and turning around and selling them for a huge profit. And still others have made money by collecting, bagging and selling, of all things…cow manure!

Rest assured, there is no better way to become "accidentally" rich, than by being keenly aware of your surroundings and also keeping your ears open. People love to brag and boast. Many times just by being a good listener, you can pick up on untapped ideas that other's are passing by.

Small demographic areas are another hidden profit arena. Do not take for granted that just because a business, product or idea exists in one area of the country, that it must exist everywhere. Sometimes being the first person to transplant a business from one area to another, can turn into a highly profitable venture.

So I dare you...can you become rich by mistake?

CONCENTRATE ON MARKETING

Be extremely focused on generating leads and closing sales, as this is the lifeblood of any business. Concentrate all your available resources on advertising, promotions, discounts, marketing, sales material creative, etc, that bring in the cash and the customers. Avoid activities that do not bring you immediate leads and sales. Why would a creative entrepreneur spend his time mopping the floor, or dusting the office furniture? It doesn't make any sense. And yet, many business owners are guilty of this very act. They concentrate heavily on hiring and managing staff, building huge overheads, and creating this "thing" of a business that they have to keep feeding...or else the empire will come tumbling down like a tower of playing cards.

By building a business that is sales-oriented and avoiding your cash and time resources on items or people that do not generate sales, you set yourself up for success. So have a crystal clear focus on marketing, prospecting, and closing sales. I would even go as far as saying that as an entrepreneur, you should be spending at least 75% of your time and energy on creating and implementing sales campaigns.

Additionally, by building a company with sales always in mind (and avoiding the huge overheads), you have a better chance of making the most amount of money in the least amount of time. Employees or mundane management activities do not bog down your efforts. In this way, you build a business that best suits your lifestyle. You make money stress-free, in a comfortable surrounding, without the worries associated with other traditional businesses.

THE BENEFITS OF THINKING SMALL

Contrary to books on the subject, as well as the gospel of stuffy bottle-glassed financial advisors that extol the virtues of "thinking big"....I'm going to turn the tables around for a second and ask you to "think small." Using "smallness" to your advantage is a tactic that is usually overlooked by most business people, but nurtured by the most creative marketing gurus!

In fact, a prime example of "thinking small" can be drawn from Sam Walton (the founder of Wal-Mart) who concentrated on opening stores in smaller towns which were not noticed by his larger competitors...until he had a huge hold on the market!

Once in a while, being small can actually attract more attention than being the biggest. Have you ever seen a tiny ad sandwiched in between larger ads? The small ad stands out from the other large ads simply because of its odd size. Here are some tips to assist you in capitalizing on the "thinking small" mindset:

• Look for small media outlets that are not overcrowded by other competitors. This way you will have a larger voice in a smaller advertising medium. Besides, small media outlets usually have smaller advertising fees...which is ideal for a bootstrap entrepreneur such as you. Here is a prime example: advertise in smaller, weekly newspapers rather than the larger dailies.

• Search out new and unconventional media sources for your advertising dollars. New will mean that it is virtually unknown, untapped....and undervalued. If your huge competitors are advertising on national cable television...you might advertise in small classified ads, give out free samples of your products, try radio commercials, or create a dynamic web site. By secretly grabbing the market with untested media campaigns you literally sideswipe your competition and knock them out of the water.

• By keeping your operating costs as low as possible (hiring cheap labor for example) you can jump into smaller markets which would not be suitable for your larger competitors. You move in quickly, grab the complete market share of a small demographic area, and then you snowball your profits by moving to the next small area! You will virtually remain untouched by your competing large allies.

WALK SOFTLY, BUT CARRY A BIG STICK

The average consumer is deluged by hundreds of advertising pitches from radio, signs, television, and junk mail on a daily basis. The messages are bold, aggressive and scream out to the poor consumers. Most of the time, the overwhelmed public just tunes out all the clutter and goes about their own lives, without being affected by the advertising messages that abound. And that is precisely why you should strive to be creative, quiet and effective with your advertising campaigns. Break through the noisy crowd with your soft, simple message!

You will have noticed by now, that I did not write a chapter specifically on overcoming objections and become a master-closing salesman. And it's not that I don't think that salesmanship is important in a business, quite the contrary I might add – I think it is imperative. It is my belief though, that selling should be performed automatically by using formulas, creative sales materials or professional, experienced sales staff – rather than by the creative entrepreneur.

My expertise is creating compelling offers and advertising them quietly with "silent salesmen." You subliminally lead your prospects to come to you and hand you over their cash. There is no screaming, "hit-them-over-the-head" type of advertising message…just a heart-piercing solution to your customer's biggest, aching problem. So don't hammer them over the head, pierce them with your arrow of focused "problem-solving." Concentrate on building effective, but quiet, advertising campaigns that will catch your customers off-guard and get them to open their wallets!

THE DILIGENT DEAL-MAKER

The strategy of creating and finalizing deals is one that is practiced by countless of our nation's most successful business people. As you move from the infancy stage of your businesses and start thinking of ways to expand your growing empire, you will most surely have to become a keen "deal-maker." These are some tips and advice that you should be aware of and be prepared to act on:

• When starting any business, have an overall, long-term view of the outcome you would like to achieve. Extend your planning horizon to 100 hundred years in the future, as this is the strategy that top Japanese companies employ.
• Be ready to purchase smaller, identical businesses as your own, and merge them to build a more efficient enterprise.
• Negotiate the most favorable prices and terms that you can, paying close attention to the small details that may give you an edge over the competition.
• Manage new businesses expertly by implementing top managers, and extracting as much income as you can during the holding period.

- You have one mouth and two ears for a reason. Listen carefully during the negotiating phase and avoid bragging about your deals until the contracts are signed.
- Take newly purchased businesses apart, and sell-off the unprofitable categories one by one. By selling pieces of a company separately, you may be able to get a larger price than selling the company as a whole.
- As a direct marketer, you will know precisely how well each advertising medium works (because you track your results) and so you should always negotiate the lowest deals you can. When you buy low, you buy smart.
- Get creative with the "selling atmosphere" when tempting sellers with your offerings…make deals in adult strip clubs, on a chartered yacht, or in a rented Ferrari for example. Did you know that more deals are closed on golf greens than in meeting rooms?
- Be diligent, work nonstop to close the deal, even if this means working 16 hours a day for seven days. Wear your opponents down with your unrelenting stamina, and tenacious negotiating stance.
- Think of yourself as a "mover and shaker." Take one business formula and transpose it to another, clone it, leverage it, group it, and expand on it to build a booming empire!
- Sometimes, it makes more sense to sell out at a huge profit rather than staying in the industry and running a business till the end of time. Grow publicity to your business and attract buyers long before you are ready to sell, this way the demand by other competing suitor's will drive your selling price up. Negotiate hard and start with a selling price that is at least 50% more than the real price you would sell out for. In fact, you should let your buyer be the first to name a price – it may be higher than what you had expected to get. Show indifference to the deal being finalized, don't seem overly hurried to close the deal, and you will ultimately get the leg up. Always keep the back door open to available buyers.

SURVIVING BUSINESS SETBACKS

There will be countless bumps along the road during the long, entrepreneurial journey that you have chosen to embark on. The economic climate will invariably change and you will have to weather many recessions. Competitor's will pop up out of the woodwork and fiercely attempt to steal away your market share. Whatever setbacks you encounter in your business life, you will have to meet them squarely and deal with them assuredly. These following words of wisdom will assist you in turning your disappointments into major reversals.

• The first rule to remember in any setback is not to panic. Keep a cool and level-minded head. Next, step back and review the situation, the causes and the available solutions. Move backwards just slightly, without showing that you are retreating or losing ground. This will give you the time to take meticulous calculations in planning your counter measures.

• After detailed solutions have been examined and all risks taken into effect, move quickly to put your attack into action. Take aggressive action without any sign of indecision, making sure that your final position moves you enough forward beyond the sticking point where you originally had found yourself in.

• During these setbacks or tough economic times, you should be increasing the time and money that you spend on marketing and prospecting. Usually during tough times, the normal businessperson becomes conservative and pulls back on all his normal marketing campaigns. Listen to my words of experience…in the tough times you should be doing just the opposite: implementing an incredible marketing blitz – coming out with your biggest guns a blazing! Network with other businesses, establish yourself as an expert in your type of business, and prospect like mad. Do e-mail, faxing, telemarketing, direct mail and any other advertising that you normally do, but INCREASE the time and budget that you usually spend.

• Your goals during adverse times will be two-fold:

1. To attract as many new prospects into your business web so that you can turn them into paying clients. Do not let your possible leads run dry, or you will run into major trouble.

2. To sell more products and/or services to your established clients. Less energy will be needed to sell to your existing clients, so work them first at a feverish pace. Contact them more frequently, with new, exciting and irresistible offers to bring in more revenues.

BECOME A SPECIALIST

As you do business over the long term you will discover that certain categories or service areas within your business will generate far more income than your other service areas combined! Often, and by accident, you will stumble across a service which will surprisingly, bring in huge sales. It is this specific service that you can turn into your flagship competitive advantage.

The advantages of being in a specialty situation like this are varied, but most importantly you can charge far more for your specialty service. If you are a regular house painter for example, you may be able to charge $50/hour, but if you specialize in faux finishing, you may be able to get away with $100/hour.

Better still, if you can convince your public audience that you are a specialist in this area, you will be able to grab the market and create a monopoly for yourself...especially if your specialty service is so rare or unique that others cannot copy you. Being a unique specialist is the best way to dominate your market and leave your competitors eating your dust!

Keep in mind, that specializing does NOT MEAN that you service only one area and that's it. You probably should offer a wide array of products or services and even add a variety of additional business sectors along the way. In the future, you may decide to eliminate certain unproductive service areas and keep only the most profitable ones. By having many alternative services, and being able to hone in on a few specialties, you can take advantage of your pure profit centers and dump your losers.

ON BEING PRODUCTIVE

As your business empire thrives and grows, you will begin to notice that your businesses will draw increasing demands on your time. You will at some point, have to become a master, peak-producing entrepreneur! Becoming more productive should not resemble any thoughts of "working more." The definition that I have created for peak production is this: *Taking the actions, and using my available assets, whether tangible or intangible, to propel me the fastest in reaching my goals and dreams.*

Once you take hold of the above definition and work it into your business systems, you will get more done and not feel like you are just "spinning your wheels."

One of the most important things that you have to realize is that each individual has his/her own peak productive hours of the day. My peak productive time is between 5 a.m. till around 2 p.m., after which my energy level drops and my creative juices start cooling down. What I do on a daily basis is attempt to do my most creative, most sales-generating, most marketing ideas, during my peak productive hours where my thinking is at its highest level. Your peak hours may be from 5 to 10 p.m., or from 12 to 4 p.m., it really doesn't matter. The key is to schedule the most significant activities within your peak productive hours.

Being more productive may also mean:
- Keeping time-robbers from stealing your precious time
- Hiring a personal assistant to handle mundane personal or business tasks
- Eliminating daily chores from your life
- Ganging up errands and doing them all at once
- Being disciplined with yourself and your schedules
- Keeping the phone off the hook while you attend to more important matters
- Returning all phone calls at the same time
- Saving all your bills and letters and opening them together, once a week
- Deciding NOT to do certain activities
- Knowing that certain activities can be put off a week, one month, or even longer
- Exercising every day, which will in turn give you extra peak performing hours

I leave you with this final thought: **the wealthiest individuals in history understand and practice the strategy of allocating their most passionate, most powerful activities during their peak productive hours.** I ask you to do the same.

LEARN WITH YOUR OWN PENNY

As you are expanding your newly created businesses, there will be times when you will say "darn, I wish I had more available funds in order to grow my business faster." What I usually like to recommend in this type of situation is: to start small, and build cautiously – from your own profits...not outside sources. The first short while of any new business should be treated as a learning experience...paying your dues in a class called "Entrepreneur 101." During this stage you will be testing, gauging the market, and making sure that your business shows a profit. This is critical, since without any leftover cash, you are basically out of business.

Starting off by borrowing from strangers, friends, relatives, or commercial investors is not the ideal position to be in. You become too worried about making your interest payments to your lenders, rather than focusing on testing the market and making sure that your idea is a viable one. Sure, there are other ways to find the necessary expansion funds: such as credit cards, personal loans, grants from the Business Development Bank of Canada, insurance companies, your suppliers, credit unions and leasing companies....

What I would like to stress here is that no amount of borrowed money can ever save a worthless idea!

Once you have an established and profitable venture...that is the precise time to consider outside sources to leverage your expansion strategies. And remember that all it takes is one brilliant idea to make money out of thin air. But money alone will not solve your business problems. Trust me, I've "been there - done that." I've mistaken cash as my savior many times in my past, and I was dead wrong each and every time. So if you are going to borrow cash, heed the following advice:

• Network in social clubs and associations to attract suitable investors, generate as much publicity as you can

• For attracting friend/relative money, try to get them offering loans on their own accord (after you cleverly hint at the proven success of your business)

• Have a business plan ready, showing consistent growth

• Seek out investors before you actually need the cash, this will make you seem less desperate

• Ask for the exact amount of money that you really need and don't get in over your head

• Deal only with investors that are interested in long-term steady growth, rather than quick, high returns

BE A RISK-TAKER

Risk is a part of our lives. In fact, due to the fact that we live, we must learn to cope with risk. Risk is everywhere, in the small actions and the large actions that we take on a daily basis. You risk every time: you get in your car, walk across the street, quit your job, get married, start a new business, take a girl home that you met in a bar! We realize that risk is involved when we jump out of our regular routine and decide to do something new or unknown. Furthermore, each individual has his/her own risk tolerance. Some people feel fine investing in unpredictable tech stocks, while others can't sleep at night unless they invest in safe government-backed bonds.

HOW TO CREATE AN UNLIMITED INCOME SITTING AT HOME IN YOUR PAJAMAS

As you head out into the expansion phase of your businesses, you have to first realize what your risk tolerance is. If you have $50,000 in savings, are you willing to risk it all in growing your business…or would you take out $10,000 and risk only this small share? Many billionaires of our time like Sam Walton of Wal-Mart and John D. Rockefeller of Standard Oil, practiced fairly cautious investment strategies, never betting their whole fortunes on one roll of the dice. They did however, risk millions of dollars to expand their businesses, many times getting into huge personal and business debt in the process.

Fear not, the key ingredient that many billionaires practiced was their careful calculation of the risks and the possible returns that they would reap. They would weigh every possible outcome, leave every exit plan open, and add flexible "plan B" alternatives into their deals. Once they were sure of their decision, there would be no hesitation, they would plunge in and move forward with great enthusiasm. Many times, the richest people in the world would indeed put up their homes or their complete savings to growing their businesses.

Therefore, understand that risk should be carefully calculated according to your tolerance level. **And recognize the fact, that if you wish to become a millionaire at some point in your life, you will have to risk hundreds of thousands of dollars. If you wish to become a billionaire, you will have to risk hundreds of millions of dollars.** I can make the following statement with absolute certainty: all super-wealthy individuals DID NOT live their lives by following the safe road! When you reach two roads that diverge in a wood, which one will you take…the safe one or the risky, less traveled one?

EXPANDING BY BEING "LIKEABLE"

This saying rings so true: "You can attract more flies with honey than you can with vinegar!" I relate this statement to the ability to lead others by being a likeable person. As you expand your companies you will have to guide others to take certain actions. You will not ascertain a high ratio of success by being a hermit, sitting alone in your home office. Great success requires a great abundance of energy. Leveraging the actions of others, who have similar thoughts and goals, is one way to achieve success. There is truth to the belief that it is easier to guide people by being nice, rather than forcing them with a gun pointed to their heads!

On the road to success, you will have to get customers, employees, lenders, suppliers, and associates to look at you favorably. By being liked, you will attract the energies and the cooperative efforts of others to assist you in reaching your goals. I would now like to highlight some of the guidelines that you should follow to win people over and get them to follow your lead.

- Remembering and using a person's name is probably the most enchanting strategy to capture someone's heart and make them like you. Use their name frequently during conversation.
- Use touch as your silent weapon to win acceptance. Use a light touch on the arm or shoulder, or a pat on the back to overcome barriers. Use this technique with caution, as some people may see this as a threat to their personal space. Read the other persons body language, gestures, and facial expressions before attempting touch.
- Smile with sincerity. Smiling repeatedly shares an aura of happiness around you.
- Be truly interested in others, be an attentive listener, ask inquiring (but not prying) questions. Push the conversation so it weighs heavily on others, so that they can talk more about themselves.
- Stroke other people's egos, ask them for their personal advice/opinions, and make them feel super significant.
- Birds of a feather - DO flock together, therefore make it a habit to relate to others on their level and through their own interests and passions.

MISCELLANEOUS EXPANSION TIPS

The myriad numbers of expansion strategies that are at your disposal are simply immeasurable. This is the exact reason that I limited the following bullet form list to the most income-generating, eye-opening strategies that I have knowledge of and expertise in. Get ready for the "expansion ride" of your life…Enjoy!

Use steady and planned expansion. Focus on making your businesses extra profitable (showing 30 – 40% year-over-year growth), without FORCING expansion too wildly and overextending yourself. Release growth slowly – DON'T PUSH IT! Know what your fixed and changing expenses are – you should be able to pull these numbers out of thin air. A healthy business is a profitable business, so think of profits first. Moreover, a healthy business is a planned business. Use planning and preparation to your advantage. You can cut a tree a lot faster and with less energy, if you spend a little more time sharpening your axe!

Expand by cutting. A concept is available to you, by which you can eliminate employees, trash unprofitable segments of your company, wipe out all unnecessary fixed costs, and end up with a more profitable and growing business. This concept is similar to cutting back a rose bush so as it can grow back stronger and fuller.

Buy existing companies. Conglomerate smaller businesses into one large thriving empire. Existing businesses already have a proven success pattern that you can research and modify. You can add your expertise, ideas, or management knowledge to further grow the newly acquired company. The new company will come with it's own customer base, so you won't be struggling from scratch to bring the company up to speed. Many businesses can be bought with seller financing (no money down) further giving you an upper advantage with the use of leverage. Because of the above advantages, it is actually SAFER to purchase an existing, successful company than building one from the ground up.

Expand globally. The shrewd businessman is not walking around with his peripheral vision cut off at the sides…he is aware of global markets, neglected markets, and foreign countries that are available as alternative areas to concentrate on. Expand your thinking, think big, don't limit yourself only to North America. Sell to Mexico, export to the tropics, import from the Orient, have your products manufactured in poorer countries where labor is more attractive and cheaper. With the advent of e-mail, the internet, world-wide couriers and faxing you can do business all over the world. You might be starting a small home-based company from your kitchen table…but you don't have to necessarily think like a small fry!

Use technology. Many of your competitors will be left in the dark, if you grab hold of the present abundance of technological devices that abound and apply them to your businesses. Things like: palm pilots, cable internet (instead of dial-up), DSL (Digital Subscriber Line) another high-speed technology, commercial telephone systems, a powerful web site, talking brochures (audio tapes or CD's), video sales presentations, can all assist you to leap-frog over competitors who have not gotten on the "technology band-wagon."

Work harder. Most people only dream of making the big money...they are not willing to pay the price to achieve success. Let me ask you a couple of questions. Would you wake up at 4:30 a.m. every Saturday and Sunday if your workload required you to? Would you work 100 hours a week to get an idea off the ground? Would you work extra hours every evening between 7 to 11 p.m. to produce your own information products business? If you answered "YES" to all of the former questions, you probably have the "entrepreneurial guts" to succeed. I'm not advocating the philosophy of "all work and no play" either, you should strive for a balanced lifestyle...but you should be prepared to work harder than the average Joe if you wish to earn more money than Joe! Leave the lotteries and the gambling for the dreamers...get down to business, work hard and MAKE YOUR DREAMS TRANSPIRE INTO REALITY.

Get Lucky. Of all the books I have read on the subject of attracting luck, and using luck to expand on your life and your business, this is what I have uncovered:

1. Keep an open mind to your surroundings, as luck will come about from bizarre sources.
2. Step out of your regular routine once in awhile.
3. Talk to a wide array of different people.
4. Try new experiences.
5. Expose yourself to different ideas or points of view.
6. Be persistent, you never know when you will be inches away from your "gold mine."
7. Practice the art of tithing—give away a portion of your profits (1-10%) to needy people or charities...the feeling of "abundance" will activate unexpected wealth to come your way.
8. Take an active stance in feeding your subconscious mind with problems that it must solve, and then leave it alone to do the work—the solution will appear as a "flash" of inspiration usually at the strangest times.

Borrow as many ideas as you can. More wealth has been made by BORROWING IDEAS, or capitalizing on undervalued opportunities, than in any other manner. Take ideas from other successful businesses and model them into your own business. Use mentors and learn from their successes and copy their ACTIONS. Borrow, combine and modify whenever you can. Watch what unsuccessful people do...and then DO THE OPPOSITE!

HOW TO CREATE AN UNLIMITED INCOME SITTING AT HOME IN YOUR PAJAMAS

Be honest. I cannot think of a better way to grow your business and generate huge sales than by employing a golden, spick-and-span work ethic. Nothing, and I mean nothing, will keep your sales orders flowing in better, than an impeccable reputation by your company as seen through your customer's eyes. Shoot for the longest, unconditional guarantees that you can. Offer only devoted, and caring after sales service…and your business will grow based on the flawless reputation that you will display. Illuminate 100% credibility and respectability at all times! Use authenticity to disarm your cynical customers! Be prepared to lose money, if it will mean keeping an honest reputation with your customer.

Beat the "feast or famine" syndrome. Every business will have it's busy and it's extremely, slow periods. A trick I know of to assist you during the hungry periods is: TO MARKET LIKE MAD DURING YOUR BUSY TIMES…this way your pipeline of prospects will be full when you reach your slow period and you will have enough leads to sell your wares to. I realize that during peak periods, it is radically difficult to also be aggressively marketing while fulfilling orders…but you have to find a way to do it – your company will depend on this for survival and growth. During boom periods, your mind will be peaking, your energy will be at its highest point…this is the perfect time to think carefully and calmly about expanding your marketing ideas. Slow periods are usually when businesspeople panic, cut marketing, cut costs in other wrong places, and get completely off course. Don't make the same mistakes.

Think more, think unique. Your chief goal as an expanding entrepreneur will be to:
1. Manufacture a larger number and higher quality of goods, and
2. Provide increased and superior services far above your competitors.

Use economies of scale to your advantage, to keep your fixed costs lower and your bottom line fatter. Strive to only sell products and services that are unique in nature, and that customers cannot get somewhere else. This will give you an immeasurable advantage. Case in point: I bet you would die to find out Cadbury's Caramilk Secret….get into the chocolate business and compete head on with them. But you can't can you? The remarkable value of being 'UNIQUE" cannot be undersold!

Expect rejection…as it WILL come. As an entrepreneur, you will constantly be creating new ideas, new services and new products. Therefore, be prepared to experience every ounce of entrepreneurial emotions that will tag along with your newfound successes. Emotions such as: fear, rejection, depression, frustration, disappointment and worry will often follow you like a shadow! I have outlined numerous solutions to these feelings throughout my book, so you should have a handful of practical ideas to overcome your adversities. Simply knowing that these adversities will be a part of the entrepreneurial lifestyle, is an uplifting experience in itself. Keep in mind that in the high-stakes business world…where your competitors will eat your first-born…you will have to show PITBULL DETERMINATION to eventually succeed! On a similar note, don't create a business that has to run smoothly at all times…as one misstep, one little boo-boo, could ruin years of hard work.

Expansion can overwhelm your employees. An often forgotten aspect of blazing expansion, is that employees will start feeling left behind in the turmoil. They may experience a feeling of being "lost" or unbalanced. Care and attention should be given to this matter. Meet with employees to discuss: the new talent that will be coming aboard, how departmental procedures will change, but most importantly, find out if there is still a feeling of cooperation within the team. As your companies' grow, employees must be able to "ride on your coattails" without weighing you down.

Enjoy your expansion success. As you move through the expansion phase, make sure to keep your responsibilities in focus. Your customers, your investors, your associates, your suppliers, your employees, and the general public, will all require your wealth to improve THEIR LIVES…so be prepared to share it and enjoy it. If you do become one of the lucky few to hit it big and make millions, make sure to slow down a little bit and enjoy what you have accomplished. Money is not a means to an end, and the person that comprehends this fact will go a long way in achieving true happiness.

Some Final Words from the Author

Well dear readers, we have reached the end of our time together. I truly hope that you have found my material both inspirational and "life changing." I have presented to you the strategies, concepts and ideas that I myself have implemented with much success. And as I have openly shared my information with you, I wish that you would find the courage and the persistence to begin applying them in your life. You shouldn't by any means, attempt to apply all the ideas at once, as this task would be Herculian in size. Bit by bit, piece by piece you should begin using my strategies to find success in your life. And be sure that success will vary from person to person. Success may mean earning $1,000,000 per year for one person. Or it may mean earning $100,000/year working only 15 hours a week, and using the remaining time to build a strong relationship or family life. Or success may mean quitting a dreary, dead-end job and being in control of your own destiny, not really caring how much money your new business brings in.

When you look at the overall picture though, you now own the most cutting-edge material ever combined in one book, that if acted upon, will bring you measurably closer to your goals and dreams. This I do not doubt. So take the necessary action to make changes in your life for the better. My book will be a complete waste, if after reading it, you put it aside and do not attempt to make any improvements at all. By knowing that true success begins by modifying your BELIEFS, and changing your ACTIONS, you will be way ahead of others in reconstructing the life of your dreams. So start by having goals, dreams, and creating daily activities. Make sure that your goals are aligned with your values. Follow your deepest passions when creating your new businesses. Above all be persistent, have a determined focus and a burning desire. Take planned action to make your dreams come true. If at first you don't succeed, this is only an indication that your plans were not sound. If you did not reach your goal of earning $100,000/year, it means you didn't take the proper actions to earn this amount of money. But more importantly, you succeeded in discovering a plan that DID NOT earn you 100K per/year. As long as you don't quit, you will have not failed. Be flexible, change your plans and try something new.

Finally, be willing to work harder than most other people. True success is elusive in nature, and is drawn out with consistent hard work, not get-rich-quick schemes or playing the lotteries. Watch the masses, and move in the opposite direction…this is the only way to find your ultimate individuality and total empowerment over your future destiny. Believe me, there is no better feeling in the world than earning your own income, signing your own pay-check, taking vacations when you want to, taking breaks when you want to, working for as long as you want to, and living life on your own terms!

In short order, I must now leave you. I feel sincerely lucky that you have allowed me to share my information with you. My work will have been a spectacular success, when I hear how you have used my advice to improve the quality of your life and those around you.

Opportunity has now led you to two roads that diverge into a wood, and she leaves you there to make your decision. I know that you will choose the right one. So good luck, and good health on your exciting journey…and may our roads cross together in the not-so-distant future!